Click really

George Fraser has done it! *Click* perf
networking so that you can build me.   ....y, and
very rich relationships in both your personal and professional
lives.

—Susan RoAne, keynote speaker and author of *How to Work a Room*®
and *The Secrets of Savvy Networking*

George Fraser is one of the best when it comes to networking.
It is his passion. That is why he is an expert and why *Click* will
help so many people who are looking to get to the next level.
He is the man!

—Stedman Graham, author, speaker, and entrepreneur

What a great book! At last, the guru of networking shares his relationship secrets with the rest of us. *Click* cuts through the myths
about networking and gives you an elegant solution to networking that is simple and easy to understand and can be applied
immediately and successfully. If you want to revolutionize the
way you network and create lasting relationships, then *Click* is
the book for you.

—Dr. Tony Alessandra, author of *The Platinum Rule* and *Charisma*

If you want to build fulfilling lifelong personal and professional
relationships, George Fraser's pearls of wisdom are yours to
treasure.

—Susan L. Taylor, editorial director, *Essence* magazine

People don't like to just be "networked." As human beings we all
appreciate a genuine connection with one another. Presented
in the spirit of truth and encouragement, George Fraser's *Click*

equips you with the tools you need to build and sustain meaningful relationships based on mutual give-and-take. *Click* is a valuable and needed guide.

—Terrie M. Williams, author of *The Personal Touch*

Success comes from people helping people. This terrific book explains how to make it all click.

—Joe Vitale, author of *The Key* and contributor to *The Secret*

Click is an essential read for anyone wishing to create connections with people that will lead to success in business and life.

—Ivan Misner, *New York Times* bestselling author and founder of BNI

Brilliantly simple and masterfully explained, the Click formula is the key to building everlasting and soulful business and personal relationships. It's a must read for anyone that is ready to reposition themselves and take their life to the next level!

—Cheryl D. Broussard, wealth lifestyle expert and bestselling author of *The Sister CEO Guide to the Law of Attraction*

Once again George Fraser does the impossible. This book should be read by anyone who has struggled to find a job, purchase a house, raise a child, launch a business, finish school, make a sale, get ahead, or do something extraordinary.

—Dennis Kimbro, author of *Think and Grow Rich: A Black Choice*

Click immediately grabs your mind and refuses to let go. Fraser brilliantly redefines the old conceptions of networking. Written with flamboyance, vigor, and zing.

—Dr. Julia Hare, national executive director, the Black Think Tank

As someone who considers George Fraser the premier expert on networking and human relationships, even I was completely blown away with his ability to, yet again, take concepts that on the surface seem obvious and add insight and wisdom to allow readers to move beyond "networking" to "clicking." *Click* should be mandatory reading for anyone wanting to enhance their personal and professional relationships in a way that is mutually beneficial and personally rewarding.

—Keith R. Wyche, president of U.S. operations,
Pitney Bowes Management Services

Click continues to position George Fraser as one of the nation's smartest and most thoughtful business thinkers. And now, with this offering, Fraser can also add to his credit: 'The Dalai Lama of ethnical business and relationship practices.' Fraser's brilliant and profound resource will no doubt positively impact the way you live, connect, and conduct business.

—Pepper Miller, president, The Hunter-Miller Group, Inc., and
coauthor of *What's Black About It?*

George Fraser is a genius, a guru, and a griot. His spin on universal relationship truths is empowering and compelling. He reminds you that when you bring your best, authentic self to a situation, you attract the best and the world is a better place for it. *Click* is both a primer and a reminder about the art and science of networking.

—Julianne Malveaux, president, Bennett College for Women

Click is a masterpiece destined to be a classic and required reading on the roads to personal and corporate success. I highly recommend this treasure chest of invaluable wisdom and practical principles guaranteed to accelerate your journey to your full potential.

—Dr. Myles Munroe, author of *The Principles and Power of Vision*

I know this is an old cliché; however, this is a must-read book. If networking is an objective, then "clicking" is the desired result! Our lives are a networking event; learn to apply these truths in your life and reap the rewards of being fulfilled and prosperous! George Fraser nailed it in *Click*, so make this book a part of your "go through life" strategy!

—Curtis Hughes, commercial vice president, Alcoa Rigid Products Division

There is no better endorsement for the power of *Click*'s principles than George Fraser's own irrefutable ability to connect with just about anybody. If George says they work, they work. Now George has shared his secrets for achieving reciprocal success with those who matter in our lives. A must read for those who want to get ahead without leaving others behind.

—Andrés Tapia, chief diversity officer/merging workforce
solutions leader, Hewitt Associates

George Fraser is the guru on how to build meaningful and lasting professional relationships. When George speaks, I listen. When George writes, I read.

—Tavis Smiley, author and television and radio host

Filled with refreshing honesty and clarity, *Click* is the wisest book on human relationships and success that I've ever read. It gets to the point and provides solid advice and action steps as it educates and entertains with the essential points of hundreds of sources of information. It's uplifting yet very realistic as it helps you answer the big questions: Who am I? Why am I here? and What should I do next? Reading this book—and following its sage advice—will help you become a better and more successful human being.

—Luke Visconti, partner and cofounder, DiversityInc

CLICK

CLICK

**Ten Truths for Building
Extraordinary Relationships**

GEORGE C. FRASER

New York Chicago San Francisco Lisbon London Madrid Mexico City
Milan New Delhi San Juan Seoul Singapore Sydney Toronto

1 2 3 4 5 6 7 8 9 10 11 12 13 14 15 16 17 18 19 20 21 22   FGR/FGR   0 9

ISBN 978-0-07-162712-2
MHID   0-07-162712-X

Interior design by Susan H. Hartman

McGraw-Hill books are available at special quantity discounts to use as premiums and sales promotions or for use in corporate training programs. To contact a representative, please visit the Contact Us pages at www.mhprofessional.com.

This book is printed on acid-free paper.

Friends are critically important because it's God's way of apologizing for your relatives.

—George C. Fraser

To those who have helped me and/or whom I have helped—
my network and connections—thousands strong and growing.

To those listed below, we've clicked!
Thank you all for being a part of my life.

Lori Adams
Roosevelt Adams
Ronald Adrine
Na'im Akbar
Nana Akpan
Bilal Akram
Alisa Alexander
S. Tyrone Alexander
Clyde Allen
James Allen
Sylvia Allen
James Amps
Adrienne Anderson
David Anderson
Sheilah Anderson
Darrell Andrews
John Appling
Alex Arnold
Eddie Arnold
Connie Atkins
Elizabeth Atkins
Angela Avant
Edwin Avant
Lillian Ayala
Ron Bachman
Pierre Bagley
Marietta Bailey
Michael Baisden
Charles Ballard
Debra Banks
Paula Banks
Don Barden
Charlene Bastien
Phyllis Batson
Bernard Beal
Christopher C. Beale
Phoebe Beasley
Robin Beckham
Dallas Lee Bell
Sam Belnavis
Phillip Berry

Kathleen Bertrand
Isisara Bey
Leon Bibb
Don Biggins
Renee Biggs
Bob Billingslea
Marvin Bishop
Tom Boles
Johnnie Booker
Alexandria J. Boone
Pepper Boyd
Steve Boyd
Jarmell Boyd-Sims
Wanda Brackins
Harlan Brandon
Camille Bridges
Lorraine Brock
Rovenia Brock
Roz Brock
Deb Brody
Bernard Bronner
Dale Bronner
Sheila Bronner
Darlene Brooks
Dennis Brooks
Fredia Brooks
Jesse Brooks
Cheryl Broussard
Daniel Brown
Duvall Brown
Jesse Brown
Les Brown
Ona Brown
Rodney Brown
Tony Brown
Wayne Brown
Paul Bryant
Beacher Buchanan
James Burgin
Charles Burkett
Marion Burns

Harvey Butler
Tyra Butler
William Byers
David Byrd
Erskine Cade
Rob Calderin
Cherie Caldwell
Craig Callé
Danny Cameron
Steve Camhi
Shirley Carmack
Andrew Carr
Bert Carrington
Anne Carter
James Carter
Kevin Carter
Julius Cartwright
Denette Casey
Jorge Castillo
Jimmy Chandler
Rachel Cheeks
Chahn Chess
Faye Childs
Michele Choi-Tai
Cynthia Christian
Joe Chubb
Andre Clark
Frank Clark
Lenny Clark
Frank Clayton
Xernona Clayton
Susie Claytor
Mack Clemmons
Linda Clemons
Ricky Clemons
Jim Clingman
Keith Clinkscales
Charles Clinton
Brent Cloud
Richard Clower
Price Cobbs

Harold Cochran
Ray Cody
Gwen Cohen
John Cole
Keith Collins
Chevonne K. Collins
Veronica Conway
Debert Cook
Denise Cook
Susan J. Cook
Barry Cooper
Margo Copeland
Cheryl Cormier
Cynthia Cousins
Maurice Cox
Paul Cox
Angela Crawford
Charlie Crawford
Henry Creel
Melvin Crenshaw
Tene Croom
James Crosby
Melvina Crowell
Cassandra Cummings
Ron Daniels
Deavra Daughtry
Leona Davenport
Hezekiah M. Davidson
Terry Davidson
Ben Davis
Chad Davis
Charise D. Davis
Denise Davis, M.D.
Greg Davis
Pat Davis
Wayne Dawson
Marla Dean
Donna DeBerry
Delxino Debriano
Suzanne dePasse
Bill Derrick
Jerry Deutsch
Billy Dexter
Harlan Diamond
Georgette Dixon
Bob Dockery
Bob Donaldson

Bill Dorsey
Julius Dorsey
Tommy Dortch
Al Dotson
Manly Dunbar
Emily Duncan
Rhoda Dunn
Dale Duransberg
Matt Durbin
Lontia Durham
Marcia Dyson
Michael Eric Dyson
Julian Earls
Jack Ebert
Henry Edwards
Turnier Esperance
Gwen Muse Evans
Jiles Everhart
William P. Evers
Stephanie Exum
Sifa Fairclough
Robert Faithful
Janice Fenn
J. R. Fenwick
Nadja Fidelia
Lourdes Figaroa
David Fitts
Rev. Floyd Flake
Carlos Fleming
Hajj Flemings
Melvin Foote
George Forbes
Chris Forgy
Benita Fortner
Gerry Foster
Sherry Foxman
George Frame
Will Frank
Bryan Franklin
Rachelle M. Franklin
Rebecca Franklin
Shirley Franklin
Ed Fraser
Edie Fraser
Joe Fraser
Kyle Fraser
Millicent Fraser

Nora Jean Fraser
Scott Fraser
Aisha Fraser-Mason
Vicky Free
Dee Dee Freeman
Joel Freeman
Shine Freeman
V. Diane Freeman
Adena Friedman
Johnny Furr, Jr.
Mildred Gaddis
Fay Gao
Willie Gary
Denise J Gatling
Jim Gelarden
Lewis Gibbs
George Gibson
Matthew Giles
Rod Gilliam
Louise Gissendaner
Shaun Givens
Marquetta Glass
Everett Glenn
John Glover
Gloria Goins
Aundra Goodrum
Bruce Gordon
Ed Gordon
Stedman Graham
Kimberly Grant
Mel Gravely
Earl Graves
Ed Gray
Monica Green
Amie Greer
Rev. Cynthia Hale
Gerri Mason Hall
Yvonne Hamilton
Julia Hare
Hill Harper
Vickie Harris
Earl Harvey
Richard Harvey
Steve Harvey
Bill Hawthorne
Lynn Hayes-Freeland
Effenus Henderson

Nina Henderson
Rockelle Henderson
Bill Hicks
Gerald Higginbotham
Hattie Hill
Joseph D. Hill
Amy Hilliard
Greg Hinton
Melody Hobson
JoAnn Holly
Heather Holmes
Pam Holmes
Bessie House
Mike House
Janice Howroyd
Marilyn F. Hubbard
Daphne C. Hudson
Orrin Hudson
Hosiah Huggins
Robert Ingram
Leon Isacc
Carl Izzi
Charmaine Jackson
Rev. Jesse Jackson
Jonathan Jackson
Rusty Jackson
Wyatt Jackson
Kevin James
Leonard James
Myra James
Johnny Jefferson
Hensley Jemmott
Rey M. Jensen
William Jiles
Damon Johns
Bob Johnson
Carolyn Johnson
Cathy-Ann Johnson
Charles Johnson
Frederick Johnson
Magic Johnson
Marilyn Johnson
Melonya Johnson
Michelle Johnson
Mike Johnson
Richard Johnson

Roger Johnson
Terry Johnson
Winston Johnson
Willie Jolley
Cynthia Jones
Jacqueline Jones
Joyce Morrow Jones
Peter Lawson Jones
Turkey Legs Jones
Zemira Jones
Derick Jordan
Vincent Jordan
Alisa Joseph
Marilyn Joseph
Oscar Joyner
Tom Joyner
Maulana Karenga
Albert Keal
Sheila Kelley
Herb Kemp
Dennis Kimbro
Charles King
Don King
Lynne King
Richard King
Tracy A. Kinslow
Carla Labat
Excell LaFayette
Ron Langston
Bob Lanier
Sharon D. Larkin
Deanna M. Latimore
Nicole Lawrence
Walter Leavy
Creighton Lee
Spike Lee
Janice Leek
Ron LeGrand
Barry Lewis
Byron Lewis
Ed Lewis
Emmanuel Lewis
Lidj Lewis
Ellen Lippman
Mike Lisman
Dustin Logan

David W M Loines
Jerry Lopes
Pat Lottier
Karen Love
Mother Love
Barbara Lowenstein
Sonya Lowery
James Lowry
Donna Brooks Lucas
E. Jeannie Maddox
Dee Magic
James Mallard
Julianne Malveaux
B'Randi Marshall
C. Sunny Martin
Franklin Martin
Henry S. Martin
Joel Martin
Sparkie Martin
Winnie Mason
Kent Matlock
Norman Mayes
Donna McClung
Quentin McCorvey
Allegra McCullough
Renee McGee
Sean McGinness
Lloyd McHamm
Punch McHamm
Wanda McKenzie
L. Londell McMillan
Darryl McMillon
Franne McNeal
Patrick Means
Gerri Warren Merrick
Sybil Meyers
Jun Mhoon
Harriett Michel
Darrell Miller
Frank Miller
Kareem Miller
Larry Miller
Pepper Miller
Scott Miller
Rhonda Mims
Maya Mitchell

Charles Modlin, M.D.
Thomas C. Monroe
Owen Montague
Marvin Montgomery
Paul Mooney
Jim Moore
Keith D. Moore
Madeleine Moore
Melba Moore
Madeleine Morel
Beverly Morgan
Marc Moriel
Faith Morris
Andrew Morrison
Chuck Morrison
Richard Muhammad
Myles Munroe
Bashira Muttalib
Hannibal Myers
M. Naseerdeen
Rodney E. Nathan
Cosette Nazon
Todd Neal
Debra Nelson
Michael Nelson
Richard Newsome
Lisa Nichols
Carl Norman
Clarence O'Banner
Shelley O'Connor
Patrick M. O'Leary
Tracy Oliver
Sam Orum
Lisa Overton
Dominic Ozanne
Creed Pannell
Jennifer Parker
Armenious Patterson
Mary Ellen Payne
Tony Peebles
Dennis Pemberton
Emma F. Pendleton
George Pendleton
Pam Perry
Coleman Peterson
Travis Peterson

Jeff Phelps
Bill Pickard
Prester Pickett
Sandrah Pilage
Arnold Pinckney
Denise Pines
Yvonne Pointer
Charles Poole
Delores Pressley
Deborah Price
Clovis Prince
Kazell Pugh
Erica Qualls
Al Quarles
Dava Range
Bunny Ransom
Darrin Redus
Bob Reed
Matt Reeder
Ilinda Reese
Ted Reid
Ken Reynolds
Bria Rice
Deanna Rice
Linda Johnson Rice
Dustin Richardson
Bridgette Ridgeway
Don Rivers
Susan RoAne
Ken Roberts
Mike Roberts
Ed Robinson
Evelyn Robinson
Stacia Robinson
Faye Rodney
Max Rodriguez
Clarence Rogers
John Rogers
Joy Lynn Rogers
Tony Rose
Felecia J. Roseburg
Clyde Rucker
Rodney Ruffin
Pat Russell-McCloud
Steve Rutherford
Derrick Rutledge

Nick Saber
Steve Saber
Georgio Sabino
Rev. Paul H. Sadler
Synthia Saint James
Ali Salahudin
Carol Sam
Khalid Samad
Rodney Sampson
Ingrid Sanders-Jones
Georgia R. Scaife
John Schambach
Brenda L Schneider
Dennis Schwartz
Alexis Scott
Darrell & Belinda Scott
George C. Scott
Robert Scott
Laura Seaburn
William Settle
Rev. Al Sharpton
Elliott Shepherd
Michael G. Shinn
Glen Shumate
Norma Sica
Luther E. Siebert
Paul Silvestri
Steve Sims
John Singleton
Julius Singleton
Brian Sisak
Ken Smikle
Tavis Smiley
Bev Smith
Clarence Smith
Curtis Smith
Herb Smith
Hilton O. Smith
Jane Smith
John Smith
Steve Smith
Wayman Smith
Dave Snyder
Ratanjit S. Sondhe
James H. Speed
Chris Spencer

Joleen Spencer
Lenny Springs
Robert St. John
Jacquie Staton
Munson Steed
Michael Steinmetz
Dave Steward
Karen Stewart
Harry Stiggers
Harold Stone
Tyrone Stoudimire
Talayah Stovall
George Subira
Stafford Sutton
Ed Swailes
Dennis Swartz
Andres Tapia
Brenda Tate
Jewel Diamond Taylor
John Taylor
Michael Taylor
Susan Taylor
William Tedford
Sabria Terry
Sabrina Terry
Carole C. Thomas
Norman Thomas
Joseph Thompson
Belva Denmark Tibbs
Sam Tidmore
Pat Tobin
Luther B. Towers
Dorita Treadwell
Rick Treadwell

Lee Triggs
Cindy Trimm
Adam Troy
Natalie V. Trueheart
Stephanie Tubbs-Jones
Chief Tunde
Iyanla Vanzant
Clara Villarosa
Luke Visconti
Sunni Walker
Robert Wallace
Charmaine Ward
Gerri Warren-Merrick
Bill Washburn
Sherita Washington
Arlene Watson
Dennis Rahim Watson
Rev. Lance Watson
Jerry Weintraub
Owen Wengard
Cornel West
Kwa David Whitaker
Al White
Chariece White
David Whitehead
Reginald J. Whitehead
Leonard Whitlow
Barbara Williams
Bruce Williams
Corky Williams
Daisey Williams
Diane Williams
Grace Williams
Greg Williams

Gregory Williams
Hadji Williams
Icy Williams
Lloyd Williams
Mary Therese Williams
McGhee Williams
Reggie Williams
Terrie Williams
Linda Coleman Willis
Travis Wills
Gwen Wilson
Julia Wilson
Lynn Wilson
Mary Wilson
Wayne Winborne
Jesse Wineberry
Debora Winfree
Glenn Winfree
Sherry Winston
Terri Winston
Maxine Witter
Dee Wood
Stephanie Wood
Clarence Wright
Frances Wright
Michael A. Wright
Keith Wyche
Kym Yancey
Carlton Yearwood
Mike Young
Ricky Young
Jonny Ray Youngblood
Sharvishia Zeigler
Howard Zoss

Contents

Acknowledgments

THIS BOOK HAS been brewing in my mind for nearly a decade, and had it not been for my family, friends, colleagues, and associates—my network—the idea for this book would have never clicked. First, I must acknowledge the Creator for His divine guidance and for allowing me to be a vessel by which He communicates His ideas.

Few authors are gifted with agents who fight hard for the right deal, the right idea. Barbara Lowenstein and Madeleine Morel are two of the best at what they do. Deborah Brody, my committed editor at McGraw-Hill, added insight, encouragement, and savvy to this project, and I was provided with the best of editorial teams.

When compiling any list of people who have been instrumental in bringing a book to life, it is usually difficult to single out one person, but not in this case. I can't think of anyone who deserves more credit than my friend, researcher, and alter ego, Elizabeth Atkins. She anticipated my every need and helped to shape my writings, ideas, thoughts, and themes into a cohesive whole. Her knowledge, sensitivity, and writing skills contributed greatly to the end product you are about to read.

Then there are those who have contributed lifelong joy as well as intellectual and moral support. Kyle and Scott, my sons and the next generation; and Jean, my wife of thirty-four years. Other special people who continue to influence me include my siblings, Edward Fraser and Emma Fraser Pendleton; my best friend, Corky Williams; my mentor, Dr. Kwa David Whitaker, Esq.; and my business partner, Greg Williams, all of whom watch my back and give all that they have, all the time. I'm eternally grateful to have such people as part of my life.

I'm also especially grateful to the following friends for their revealing thoughts: Veronica Conway, Craig Callé, Rachelle Franklin, Dr. Joel Freeman, Hattie Hill, Orrin Hudson, Darrell Miller, Luke Visconti, Terrie Williams, and Kym Yancey. Their inspiring stories pepper this book with peeks into their private lives that click on and off, in one form or another.

The writing of a book while speaking 140 times per year and traveling 250,000 miles is difficult, especially if you are trying to run a thriving publishing, Internet, and special events business. Running a business is difficult at best when you are operating on all cylinders, let alone when you are preoccupied with a major project. The fact of the matter is that my team really runs the business: Greg Williams, Jarmell Boyd-Sims, Sunni Walker, Lisa Overton, Dustin Richardson, Bria Rice, Kyle Fraser, Duvall Brown, Heather Holmes, Lontia Durham, Bob Donaldson, and the late Hubert Payne (God rest his soul). Thank you all for stepping in and stepping up when it really mattered.

Last, I believe it is important to recognize the giants of networking in America and the great thinkers and contributors to our understanding of connectedness, the science of human relationships, and happiness. They include Na'im Akbar, Mac Anderson, Stephen Covey, Keith Ferrazzi, Daniel Gilbert, Jeffery Gitomer, Malcolm Gladwell, Daniel Goleman, Stedman Graham, Earl

Graves, T. D. Jakes, Maulana Karenga, Harvey Mackey, Ivan Misner, Susan RoAne, Anthony Robbins, Jim Rohn, Susan Taylor, Brian Tracy, Dr. Joe Bitale, and the great John C. Maxwell. Their words and ideas have contributed greatly to shaping my own thoughts. Surely many more will follow their example and be infected by their exuberant spirit.

This extensive list barely scratches the surface of the many people who have influenced me and helped me to grow. I am ever so grateful for the many who have given so much to enrich my life through the process of networking . . . connecting . . . then clicking!

Introduction

Life is not measured by the number of breaths we take,

but by the moments that take our breath away.

—George Carlin

DOES THE IDEA of networking make you cringe?

Does the word conjure up awkward images of standing alone at a mandatory company meeting that's bustling with people who all seem to know each other—and when you do make small talk with someone, it feels fake and self-serving? Or does the word remind you of ruthless men and women you've met who seem like they're competing on a TV reality show called *Extreme Networking*? They act like the first contestant to meet, impress, and get promoted by the CEO earns a luxury corner office, a fat salary, and an express pass up the company ladder. And they'll do anything to win.

Perhaps the term *networking* reminds you of other folks who are betting on the business card game to hit their career jackpot.

You know the ones: you meet them at conferences, at receptions, and even in elevators. They pass out business cards like they're blackjack dealers, demanding your card in exchange. Then these one-armed bandits call weeks or months later, as if they've fed your business card into a slot machine, and your name suddenly popped up, three-in-a-row, in the little windows. *Cha-ching!*

They call you, trying to cash in on your contacts. These strangers boldly ask you to get them a job, purchase something from them, contribute to their nonprofit organization—even invest your time and energy as their mentor—yet they barely know you or you them.

Networking on a personal level can feel just as ruthless. If you're a single woman, for example, and you're hoping to meet Mr. Right, a professional conference can feel as much like a meat market as a nightclub. It may seem like everyone is out to get something, and that something might be you—personally or professionally.

For those of you for whom any of the above scenarios rouses a groan of recognition, I'm going to share new insights that can transform your every negative twinge about networking into something beautiful and powerful. As I've studied the laboratory of humanity and researched attitudes about networking, I've pinpointed Ten Truths for connecting and ultimately "clicking" with people. With these insider secrets, you'll be able to build extraordinary relationships. You'll feel reconnected with men and women in a world where technology, corporate downsizing, and distrust are disconnecting us more and more every day.

The first question I had to ask myself regarding this disconnection and social isolation I see in people is, why does it even exist? The culprits include communication technology, the Internet, suburban sprawl, two-career families, and television. We used to all gather as families around the one TV or radio in a home for much of our social interaction, but as television and radio programming quickly migrates from the family room onto desktops, laptops, cell phones, portable video game players, and iPods, it forces us into isolation.

What can be done? According to Harvard University professor Robert Putnam, author of the book *Bowling Alone*, "We can solve this problem fairly easily by simply getting more involved in our communities and spending more time with family and friends. Family-friendly workplaces would help too. Reaching out to a neighbor or connecting with a long-lost pal—even having a picnic or two could just save your life."

Here's a novel idea. A pet site like Dogster.com "is another way for humans to connect," writes Malak Hamive of *Newsweek*. "Owners, who communicate with one another mainly in the voices of their animals, usually wind up making human friends."

That's how my wife of thirty-four years, Jean, connected with almost everyone in our cluster home development. While walking Bandit, our twelve-year-old shih tzu, Jean met other dog lovers, joggers who love dogs, walkers who love dogs, and other dogs and cats who love dogs. Very quickly, Jean knew everybody and their business. Our home soon became animal and information central; a few deer even dropped by to eat our geraniums, catch up, and sniff Bandit.

"Connections with other people affect not only the quality of our lives but also our survival," writes Dean Ornish, M.D., in his book *Love and Survival*. "Study after study finds that people who feel lonely are many times more likely to get cardiovascular disease than those who have a strong sense of community. I'm not aware of any other factor in medicine—not diet, not smoking, not exercise, not genetics, not drugs, not surgery—that has a greater impact on our quality of life, incidence of illness and premature death."

Throughout *Click*, you'll find sparkling gems of truth that will enable you to make magic happen and connect on every level of your life. These Truths are simple yet profound. They're about changing the way you network so that you connect with people on a level that is much deeper and more productive than exchanging business cards. I'm talking about the kinds of personal connections that draw two or more people together for an extraordinary marriage, a lifelong friendship, a winning team, or a business relationship that creates an innovative product that enriches people's lives. Some folks achieve this through the activity of networking, which leads to a great connection that will click. But most relationships seem to fall short.

I can best illustrate this point if you think of a key that is precisely cut to fit a particular lock. When you insert that key into the lock, and you turn the key, it clicks and the door opens. We can view our relationships the same way. A combination lock requires knowing the three numbers in perfect sequence so that the lock opens with a definitive click. The fullness of a relationship can open up to us just as easily and gracefully, or with similar ease.

In this book, I will explain exactly how you can click with people and enjoy extraordinary relationships. To do that, I will show that networking is the ongoing, lifelong activity of identifying those with whom you wish to build new relationships; connecting is the developmental process of finding, cultivating, nurturing, and building relationships; and clicking is when at least two people add special value to each other and create synergy. My main goal is to help you connect and click with more people in business and in life.

Chemistry, Fit, and Timing

We click when the following three variables align with another person's: chemistry, fit, and timing. This combination forms the DNA of all relationships, especially those we enjoy with good friends, partners, marriages, winning teams, and organizations.

Are there public figures, companies, and brands that we click with? Absolutely! Advertising and public relations are part of the equation, but even so, these brands and people wow us and we buy into what they are selling, saying, or doing. People like Oprah Winfrey, Bill Clinton, Tiger Woods, Julia Roberts, Bono, and Barack Obama all have it. And whether it's the innovation of Apple, the customer service of Nordstrom, the wholesomeness of Disney, or the rebelliousness of Harley Davidson, these companies and brands all inspire a loyalty based on their ability to connect with their customer.

To explore this idea of a "formula" for relationships, I spent a day with Dr. Lidia Cucurull, a Ph.D. in physics and math. A scientist at the Joint Center for Satellite Data Assimilation, in Washington, D.C., she was so moved by the concept of *Click* that she helped me formulate the three variables of a relationship—chemistry, fit, and timing—into the following equation:

$$C^2 \times F \times \sqrt{T} = CL$$

C^2: Chemistry is squared because it is the most important variable and therefore is heavily weighted in the equation. It is a variable over which we have some control.

$\times$: $\times$ is used instead of $+$ because $\times$ means that all variables must be present to achieve CL, or "Click."

F: Fit is heavily influenced by trust and common goals.

$\sqrt{\textbf{T}}$: Timing is square rooted because it has the least value or weight and can be managed or controlled to a great extent.

Chemistry involves: emotions, aura, charisma, posture, energy, physiology, smell (pheromones), gut feelings, clothing, appearance, humor, and temperament.

Fit pertains to: common goals and objectives, shared values and mores, shared experiences, shared circumstances, shared projects, shared vision/mission, high levels of trust, common interests, common focus, or unusual circumstances.

Timing can be: planned, managed, and it can relate to circumstances and happenstance.

From Networking to Clicking

I am sharing this equation and these Truths because I want to help you master your ability to create wonderful relationships in your personal and professional lives. Networking, as I have been saying for more than three decades, is the way to achieve that. However, after observing all that is wrong with the way we network, and after studying how successful people click to form phenomenal relationships, partnerships, and teams, I am taking the concept of networking to a much higher level.

My goal with this book is to correct networking wrongs and show you exactly what I do to connect and click with so many great people, to lay out for you the very thing that inspires so many men and women across America and the world who look to me for advice. I want to change the opinions of all those who cringe when they hear the word *networking*. I want to show people how to network in a better way and how to get a better result.

The frank confessions of networking gone wrong found in this book, deal a devastating blow to me as someone who's invested three decades of my life to studying and praising the gospel of this subject. I do this because it is my passion and my purpose to teach people how to tap into the richest resource on the planet—other people—to achieve goals and share their talents in business and in life. Yet the most common mistake that people make in networking is to focus on their own needs, without finding a way to serve, to give or to add value to the person they've identified to meet.

On top of that, many people view networking as the small talk that's just a ploy to butter someone up to get something. Most people loathe small talk. It feels trite and awkward. And it reinforces the feeling that networking is just a self-serving game in which people use, and in some cases, abuse each other, or as I once heard someone say, "Networking is the unpleasant task of trading favors with strangers."

Why is networking and thus building potent relationships that click so important to you personally? Because well-developed networks deliver three unique advantages, according to Brian Uzzi and Shannon Dunlap in their *Harvard Business Review* article, "How to Build Your Network": private information, access to diverse skill sets, and access to power networks.

The first advantage is the private information gathered from personal contacts who can offer something unique that cannot be found in the public domain; most serious business deals and job opportunities are the result of private information. My last three leadership positions, with Procter & Gamble, United Way, and the Ford Motor Company, all came as a result of close and trusted personal relationships with friends. These are all people I had originally met at conferences, trade shows, social events, and/or informal shared activities such as volunteering for United Negro College Fund (UNCF), The Great Lakes Theater Festival, or the Cleveland Ballet.

The second major advantage of a network of diverse connections is immediate access to a broad array of skill sets. Most of my best ideas and results have come from filtering my thoughts through a wide variety of skilled professionals in my network. Whether it's a graphic design theme for my PowerNetworking Conference or a new book idea, I seek input from a "kitchen cabinet" of people I know, like, and trust. It was Linus Pauling, the double Nobel Prize winner, who said, "The best way to have a good idea is to have a lot of ideas." Said another way, your key to success will be directly related to your willingness to ask people for help. And whomever you're asking for help is your network. Transcending your natural skill limitations through others will significantly increase your success ratio.

The final advantage of a network of diverse connections with whom you click is your ability to become a leader and/or power broker. According to Uzzi and Dunlap, "new age 'power' is now more embedded in a flatter organization as opposed to being at the top of the pyramid." So, people like me who are not high profile within the community can still be effective and be considered a power broker. Why? Because I've used my strong interpersonal skills to develop trusting relationships with key people who influence specific intellectual, social, civic, and business groups. Thus I've helped to connect the separate clusters, synthesize opposing points of view, and ultimately stimulate collaboration and contribute to the resolution of key issues among these independent and culturally diverse groups. My annual PowerNetworking Conference and PBS personality Tavis Smiley's State of the Black Union symposium are good examples of the manifestation of this power through a net-

> *"The best way to have a good idea is to have a lot of ideas."*
>
> —Nobel Prize winner
> Linus Pauling

work of diverse connections. To that end, great hope is available for anyone who possesses the requisite interpersonal skills to lead, have power, and therefore effect change, regardless of where he or she is in the social, civic, or business hierarchy.

My modest beginnings prove this point. I was orphaned at four and grew up in foster homes all my life. Although I was encouraged to quit school and go to work, I graduated from Thomas Edison Vocational High School in 1963; I had a diploma in cabinet making because I was not considered college material. I had little hope and no expectations. I had no special skills and no elite network of contacts to tap into. What I had, but didn't know at the time, were strong interpersonal skills that would facilitate every job offer I ever received, every promotion I ever earned, and every friend I would ever need to eventually become a top earner and a successful businessman at the very pinnacle of my evolving profession.

Within thirty years, I had become a master networker, meeting thousands of people along the way, connecting with many, and clicking with the relative few who would change my life as I would change theirs. We didn't know at the time why the synergies of our newfound relationship worked so well; we just knew we clicked on many levels. We wanted many of the same things in life; we shared common interests and common ground, and our aspirations and inspirations intersected. Several hundred of those relationships from work, family, and the community are still alive, well, and productive today.

Connecting with people determines which business deals get done, who gets elected, who becomes a star, which new drugs are prescribed, who gets promoted, who you'll marry, and who buries you. Connecting, when done with finesse, can spark spectacular partnerships. It can link groups, communities, friends, mentors, bosses, and employees. No doubt about it, connecting makes the business world go round: no less than 85 percent of all jobs are secured through networking, connecting, and, ultimately, clicking.

It is my desire to fix whatever might be wrong with the way many people network. It's my goal to make you feel good when you hear the word *networking*. Instead of cringing, I want you to smile with the knowledge that networking is taking your life to a better place, and helping others as a result.

The very folks who tell me that networking makes them cringe are the ones who—upon further conversation—reveal that their networking techniques are profoundly flawed. These men and women—from everyday folks to CEOs—provide powerful observations in my human laboratory. Now I'm ready to report my findings to you.

Networking Versus Connecting

Let's start with the difference between "networking" and "connecting." Think of connecting/clicking as the Ph.D. of networking. If networking is the handshake and the smile, then connecting/clicking are the heartfelt feeling, the trust, and the exciting burst of energy that sparks when we meet someone who shares our values, can add value, or takes interest by questioning our reasoning and challenges us.

In contrast, many networking relationships are flimsy because they feel self-serving. The ability to connect is blocked by a lack of common ground and shared values, principles, and goals. This occurs because you are interacting with someone whose job allows him or her to control something that you want—a job, a contract, etc. As soon as that situation disintegrates, nothing remains to sustain a relationship. In effect, this relationship is motivated by the deal, the promotion, the dollars. Approaching relationships from this mind-set is all about take, take, take for me, me, me. Perhaps this is why a Gallup study showed that almost 50 percent of people polled say the most nagging aspect of networking is "wasting time" with people who may lack the skills, resources, or desire to help us.

Instead, Stephen Covey, author of *The 7 Habits of Highly Effective People*, recommends that the first step to advancing on any level begins with studying a new way of thinking and incorporating a new model for success into the way we pursue and cultivate relationships. Covey writes, "If you want to make minor, incremental changes and improvements, work on practices, behavior, or attitude. But if you want to make significant, quantum improvements, work on paradigms."

In this book, I offer you that paradigm. Below is a chart to help you compare and contrast the differences between what most people call networking and what I call connecting/clicking.

Connecting/Clicking is . . .	Networking often is . . .
Sharing common ground	**Superficial**
You tend to bond with those who have similar dislikes and experiences regarding people, places, and things.	*Your relationship may never reveal similar likes or go deeper than friendly chit-chat.*
Value-based	**Goal-based**
You team up with people who share your values and principles. You focus on matters of the heart before goals in the head.	*You interact with someone to search for leads, make a deal, get a job, etc.*

Connecting/Clicking is . . .	**Networking often is . . .**
Assumed trust	**Earned trust**
You believe in the good of people, first.	*You are guarded until people prove themselves trustworthy.*
Synergistic	**Compromise**
Both people bring something to help the other; together your efforts don't make two, but eleven!	*Two people come together; I give up something, and you give up something, and together we have one-and-a-half.*
Relational	**Transactional**
Your relationship is about the person: building rapport, what you can do to enhance them or help others.	*Your relationship is about the deal, exchange of cards, the immediate sale, the transaction.*
Mutually beneficial	**Often one-sided**
Both parties enter the relationship feeling enthusiastic and excited about projects and profits that they will create together.	*One person pursues another with the hope of landing a job, making the sale, etc.*
A conscious, strategic process	**A haphazard process**
You choose the people with whom you would like to connect and stay open to attracting like-minded colleagues.	*You cast a wide net hoping for a "chance" introduction to someone who can help you.*
Holistic	**Often materialistic**
You connect with people with the mutual goal of helping others.	*You cultivate a relationship with your eye on a thing(s).*

Connecting/Clicking is . . .	Networking often is . . .
Multidimensional	**One-dimensional**
You win, I win, others win. Resources and ideas are shared to help a lot of people.	*It's all about me getting what I can from you.*
A long-term commitment	**Temporary**
You plan to cultivate a meaningful relationship over time, by sowing seeds.	*The relationship ends when the deal is done.*

Think about how the above dynamics played out the last time you met someone new while networking. Chances are, your interaction began with a strong handshake, a warm smile, eye contact, and a short, punchy introduction about fifteen seconds long. Add good listening skills, and your networking activity shifts into high gear. All of the habits listed in the chart tell other people they are interesting and special.

Now think about how you move the conversation beyond the weather and sports scores when you are trying to connect with someone new. You evaluate them through your invisible lens of chemistry, fit, and timing:

You play golf? Oh I golf, too.
You're from Chicago? So am I.
You're a vegetarian? So am I.
You have twins? Me, too.
You're going to start a charter school? So am I.

This common ground inspires conversations, friendships, and business deals. Why? Because when we meet someone who has something in common with us, it creates comfort and builds trust. With speed and sincerity, you communicate your goals and values; people who resonate to your intent will respond.

And if you establish a connected relationship, you can reap tremendous benefits. Your new partner will share opportunities, an empathetic ear, and fresh ideas. The more common ground you have, the better the fit and the higher the trust level. And the higher the trust level, the more a person is willing to share key contacts, information, and resources.

The "Click" equation, in conjunction with the Truths, is a powerful formula for creating phenomenal relationships in your life and evaluating relationships that do not work. In essence, it is the DNA to build on, attract, and nurture relationships that are fulfilling, productive, and beneficial to you, the other person, and others. So let's get started. First, think about what networking means to you. For most people, networking starts with the premise: "I'm going to get something out of this relationship."

But that's backward. You have to flip it around and network with the goal of "I'm going to give something in this relationship."

So let's get started. First, think about what networking means to you. For most people, networking starts with the premise: "I'm going to get something out of this relationship."

The goal of all networking is to find a human connection and then *add value.* Those two little words spell rocket fuel when it comes to connecting. Now say it out loud: "I want to add value to every person and situation I encounter." And when you meet someone new, ask, "How can I use my talents, connections, and resources to enhance this person's business and/or life?"

This is Truth #3: Love, Serve, Give, and Add Value—First! Incorporating this truth into your life allows you to network and connect for the right reasons. It reminds you that in order to get, you must give first. Then, whatever you give sparkles back on you a thousand fold.

In this book, you'll find intriguing anecdotes from accomplished men and women who practice these Truths as the secrets for their success in business and in life. With me they share real-life—and sometimes intimate—experiences that reflect the power of my Ten Truths, even if the outcome is embarrassing, humbling, or just plain ugly.

International business consultant Hattie Hill lives by all Ten Truths, including the one about giving first. And when she encounters someone who doesn't exhibit the give first attitude, she feels a disconnect. "When I meet someone who clearly just wants to take, take, take whatever they think they can get from me," says Dallas-based Hill, "I decide it's time to prune this person from my inner circle, or my relationship tree. A great relationship is a connection in which I share with you, you share with me, and together we create something wonderful for everybody."

When Hattie talks about pruning, she's not referring to her garden. She's touting Truth #5: Bless Them and Release Them. If our relationships form a tree of life, then you've got to snip the branches that are a toxic drain on your strength and ability to grow the most succulent fruit. This is rooted in one of my favorite Fraser-isms: If you want to change your life, change your relationships. At some point we realize that we can't spend major time with minor people.

Writer Nina Brown took that to heart, as she explains in Truth #5, by pruning her relationship tree of its most luscious fruit: her lover. At first he looked and tasted like a sweet, golden apple. But as time always tells the truth about people, her lover began to bare his bitter spots. And Nina lost her appetite for him. "If a lover is our mirror image," Nina says, "then Damion reflected some things that I needed to change about myself. By cutting him loose, I made room to grow stronger, healthier relationships, starting with myself. In fact, the other day someone said, 'You're glowing! Are you in love?' And I realized, 'Yes, with the new person I'm becoming by living these Ten Truths.' "

From your personal life to your professional persona, the Ten Truths for connecting with people play out in ways that make your reputation gleam in the eyes of the powers-that-be.

Craig Callé learned that the awkward way during a high-stakes business trip to Scotland. As the assistant to the CEO of an international investment company, Callé was staying at the most luxurious hotel in town. In the midst of chauffeured cars, a private jet, and big-money negotiations, Callé got a reminder of the platinum rule that's Truth #7: Tailor Your Relationships for the Perfect Fit. "My behavior in this particular situation taught me an unwritten, unspoken point of etiquette," says the San Francisco founder of Common.Net. "It's something that, while small and even trivial to others at the time, was something that I incorporated into our [Callé and his CEO's] relationship . . . to connect the dots, so I could treat him as he wished to be treated."

Veronica Conway approaches her fairytale romance with the same idea, as she lives Truth #6: Trust First; Distrust Must Be Earned. But how do you do that when both the man and the woman are so attractive, powerful, and prominent—that flirtatious admirers are fawning at every turn? The answer is trust, which is the bedrock of every relationship. But that can be a challenge even for couples whose connection is so intense that "time stood still" when they met. Veronica offers some unusual insights into how she's learned to trust.

"You can't trust another person until you fully trust yourself," she says. "Trust is an inside-out job. Because once you trust yourself, you don't need to trust others. I need to trust me and how I respond with my skills and abilities to whatever life brings. When you trust yourself, and you trust the process of life, that eliminates that whole question of 'Do I trust you?' "

She treats relationships with the kind of open mind that exemplifies Truth #9: Be Open to Everything and Attached to Nothing; the Best Idea Wins. That reinforces one of my favorite quotes from leadership expert John Maxwell, and what is Truth #10: It Takes Teamwork to Make the Dream Work.

Because you cannot do this alone, one is not a sufficient number to achieve greatness. In fact, all entrepreneurship, job searches, and upward mobility are networking initiatives. And the key to success is directly related to your willingness to ask for help from people you trust, and who believe in you. You cannot attain, sustain, or maintain success without working with and through all kinds of people. You must connect to reach success.

It's Time to Reconnect

I'm making an urgent call for all of us to reconnect in our disconnected world. Everything from our health to our life spans to our careers to our personal happiness depends on our ability to share fulfilling relationships with friends, family, lovers, colleagues, clients, and even strangers. In fact, scientific research proves that we catch fewer colds, we feel happier, we make more money, and we even live longer when we enjoy great relationships.

But the very technology that's supposed to connect us so quickly and conveniently—is actually disconnecting us from human contact. Need proof? Look around. Look around many restaurants at lunchtime and you'll see folks sitting together, but everybody's talking into cell phones or typing into text message devices. They're using beeping, blinking gadgets to disconnect from the people around them.

Not only that, but we spend less time together. Corporate downsizing often forces one person to do the work of three. That means longer hours and lunching alone at one's desk. Working parents, business travelers, and too many others are chronically sleep-deprived. That causes withdrawal and depression.

We distrust and shun people. Crime, corporate scandals, and competition have obliterated the belief that "a friend of yours is a friend of mine." I witness the ravages of this everywhere I go, from crowded restaurants to bustling offices to jam-packed elevators. I see people who are emotionally, physically, and spiritually disconnected from each other. This makes my heart ache: the more technologically connected we become, the more disconnected we are as people.

How can we reverse this trend and progress forward into a life that's rich with emotional, spiritual, and financial reward? By connecting to create deep, powerful, long-lasting relationships. So please study and apply my Ten Truths to your life. They are the building blocks of extraordinary relationships that will help you get reconnected in our disconnected world. And you'll never cringe again when you hear the word *networking*. In fact, you'll smile, because you'll be living and loving the abundant success and happiness of connecting and clicking with more and more people.

CLICK

PART 1

CHEMISTRY

Chemistry *noun*
1. the interaction of one personality with another
2. sympathetic understanding; rapport
3. any or all of the elements that make up something

Adapted from the *Random House Unabridged Dictionary*, © Random House, Inc., 2006.

Chemistry is the magic mixture of emotions, intuition, and attraction that sparks bonds between us in business, life, and love. In the awesome laboratory of life, chemistry is that intangible energy that makes friendships sparkle, marriages sizzle, professional partnerships prosper, and teams triumph.

Chemistry is the most powerful component in relationships because it provides the initial spark when we click. Either you have it with someone or you don't; chemistry cannot be fabricated. And the only way to measure it is with a very unscientific hunch: you know it when you feel it.

But try to wrap words around this phenomenon we call chemistry. Try to articulate why you clicked with a spouse, a business partner, a best friend, or a teammate. Chances are, you'll stumble on oversimplifications such as, "It just feels right," or "I can't put my finger on it; I just knew the minute I met him that we belonged together."

Your words may be elusive, but your feelings will confirm that chemistry is working powerfully in your relationships. So how do we define chemistry? It is the perfect fusion of many elements: being authentic, communicating honestly, giving and releasing, sharing cultural affinity, values, and point of view, and pampering the people with whom we enjoy these dynamics.

Truths #1, 2, 3, and 4 reveal the formula for creating this synergy.

To begin, Truth #1: Be Authentic, urges you to be true to yourself and to others. That means first indulging your passion for doing what you love; that will guide you to your purpose. For example, if you are a stockbroker who dreams of becoming a painter, and you follow your heart, then your passionate sense of purpose will activate the universe's powerful law of attraction to deliver rich relationships and mind-blowing prosperity. Then, when you share your authentic self in those relationships, you are making a positive impact on the world.

Truth #2: Communicate with Your Heart, enables you to listen carefully and speak sincerely with words that express how you really feel. As a result, your honesty strikes a powerful chord in others; it creates chemical reactions within us that cement relationships. This endears people to you because your integrity acts as a mighty magnet to draw other honest communicators into your life.

Next, take this one awesome step further with Truth #3: Love, Serve, Give, and Add Value—First! Be generous in friendships, in business, in romance, always focusing on how you can uplift and inspire others. Being authentic, while speaking from your heart, will enable you to share your ideas, your love, and your resources in ways that enrich your life beyond measure. Truth #3 is a biblical truth; what you invest in others enriches your life with opulent dividends.

Last, Truth #4: Nurture Your Relationships—and Yourself, is your insurance to protect and prolong the magic after you click with someone. When you pamper your relationships with kind words, thoughtful actions, and attention to detail, you show each person that you are making a long-term commitment to his or her happiness and prosperity.

So now, when you try to express that special something that makes you click with your best friend, your business partner, or your lover, you'll know the answer. It is these four Truths—they make us click!

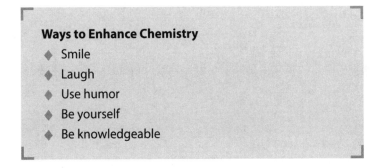

Ways to Enhance Chemistry
- Smile
- Laugh
- Use humor
- Be yourself
- Be knowledgeable

Be Authentic

Man's main task in life is to give birth to himself.

—Erich Fromm

WE EACH PLAY one role in the huge cast of humanity live on the stage of life every day; this is not a dress rehearsal. So we must act in a way that is mutually beneficial to everyone. You can unleash infinite powers within by following your purpose and passion. Smile. Be yourself, and know that your work is helping people; this will boost your confidence. And this, in turn, will create a phenomenal performance that helps many people.

"In your life you are always at one of three points: heading into a storm, in the midst of a storm, or coming out of a storm," says Rev. Jeremiah Wright of Trinity United Church of Christ.

Franne McNeal was in the midst of a storm—breast cancer . . . then a stroke. She faced the traumatic ordeal of a radical mastectomy and physical therapy to learn how to walk again.

This tall, impeccably groomed, and statuesque beauty has the voice of a network news anchor, a smile that can light up a room, and a brilliance that helped her sail through one of America's elite Ivy League universities. Amazingly, despite her health crisis, she maintains the same sense of humor and passionate purpose that impressed me years ago.

We clicked at a book signing party at a home in Pittsburgh. I loved her entrepreneurial zeal and her sincere interest in my interests. She wanted to know more, a lot more, about networking.

Shortly after we met, Franne left Pittsburgh for Philadelphia. We remained connected through e-mail, occasional phone calls, and ultimately a generous proposition: "Come to Philadelphia," she said, "give a speech on networking, and I'll put the whole thing together for you, if you will spend some time teaching, guiding, and mentoring me on the activity of networking . . . no strings attached."

The deal was on. Franne found sponsors, a corporate venue, and—through her superior public relations skills and sheer charisma—hundreds of people to attend. In doing so, Franne created the classic win-win-win-win situation. She won on two levels: she earned a profit, then spent one-on-one coaching time with me. I won, too, because I got to speak and sell books. On top of that, the hundreds of people who attended the event won by hearing my speech about how to improve their lives by networking. And the corporate sponsors won by getting positive community-based coverage . . . Click!

Sharing creates bonding with people. Franne and I shared our resources. And in doing so, we formed a bond that enables us to enjoy a great relationship many years later. In hindsight, we clicked because the chemistry, fit, and timing all synchronized for a long-term friendship and business relationship to blossom. Franne was easy to talk to, and she always had a ready smile and an attentive ear. So, along with her natural elegance, good chemistry cemented our relationship. Our fit related to our common interest in networking and entrepreneurial endeavors. Fit also came into play because she wanted to plan an event, and my appearance and speech became that event. And the timing was just right because she was at a stage of her career that required a crash course in better networking, and I am always eager to participate in a speaking engagement and to help people learn.

My initial encounter with Franne underscored three qualities that I admire in her: she is strong willed; she is authentic; and she is a risk-taker. These characteristics will undoubtedly enable her to navigate her personal storm and sail into calmer waters very soon. There, she will be looking for the next risk that will take her even closer to her sense of purpose—serving others and helping them to win.

As a highly respected entrepreneur, Franne is a master risk-taker. But when she applies that same trait to her personal relationships, she knows she's treading in uncertain waters. Franne shares her authentic self, without fearing that people will not like her for keeping it real. As a result, her courage is the essence of being authentic in a world where too many people "perform" so that others will share business deals, friendship, and romance with them. They "act" on the stage of life in ways that impress with falseness. Franne McNeal does the opposite, and she enjoys great success in her personal and professional relationships as a result.

"I'm probably better in business relationships because it's easier for me to bring to the table explicit contracting," the Princeton University graduate says from her office in Philadelphia. The celebrated business coach admits that her "clinical approach" to relationships inspires her to constantly "paraphrase and check for understanding" as if the two parties were in a coaching session or signing a contract. Sometimes, Franne says, this quest for clarity strikes people as pushy and controlling.

She is practicing what is preached by Po Bronson, author of *What Should I Do with My Life?* "People don't succeed by migrating to a 'hot' industry or by adopting a particular career-guiding mantra," Bronson writes. "They thrive by focusing on the question of who they really are—and connecting that to the work they truly love."

Franne is doing just that. "When I dissect my stronger friendships with my girlfriends, they tell me that my authentic listening and the authentic space that I give for them to be them are part of what makes me attractive," says the forty-five-year-old CEO of the business coaching firm, HR Energy. "My communication style allows other people to express themselves in terms of what they value and need. Many people are not often asked what it is that they value, and many people are not listened to when they think of the answer."

Franne's commitment to showing her authentic self is so powerful, it enchanted another entrepreneur during a business event in New York City. Magic Johnson had just delivered a keynote speech about his business ventures, when Franne charged into the buffet line. But it was moving slowly, and she felt impatient. "I was hungry and tired and I might have said, 'I wish people would hurry up because they're between me and my turkey.' "

That's when the man in front of her turned around. His words and his body language had an immediate calming effect on Franne's fast-paced, goal-oriented approach to getting her meal. The man was a stranger, but she felt an immediate, magical connection with him.

"His pacing is different than mine," Franne says. "He's smoother, calmer. I was there with the purpose of wolfing down my turkey sandwich, and he was much more like, 'How did you like the event? What did you think of Magic?' In terms of the vibe, he created a very welcoming space that shifted without making me feel pushed." The connection was so strong that this man became Franne's business associate!

"In our relationship, we're the yin and the yang. I am the push. He has a more relaxed relationship style. When I'm talking about goals, roles, responsibilities, bing, bing, bing," she says playfully to imitate her quick speaking style. "He is like, 'How about we actually look at each other and smile first?' He forces me to do the proverbial stopping and smelling the roses, slowing down, because everything isn't about accomplishing something at the highest level, the fastest way. I'm working on this."

Of course, every relationship has friction. For Franne and her partner—who see each other twice a month because he lives in New York and she lives in Philadelphia—their communication styles sometimes clash. "Sometimes, I'm just thinking, 'Just do what I ask you to do!' " she says. "Then, having huffed and puffed for a minute or two, I come to my senses."

Ironically, it was his no-pressure business style that impressed Franne in the beginning. After the Magic Johnson event in New York, at which Franne had said she needed a new website for her business, he bedazzled her with a presentation about how his graphic design company could help her.

"He had gone the extra mile. He had looked at some of the work on my website. He had done one or two markups. And I remember that as he showed me what he could do, as a potential client, I felt as if, 'Wow, he's treating me as if I'm already a client and he's showing me his best work. I'm being treated with kindness and a gift.' "

Now Franne and her partner actually do business presentations as a team, which enables them to travel and spend more time together. "Doing business with your best friend takes tremendous trust," Franne says. "I trust him with my best self as well as my worst self, and I'm pretty protective of whom I show my worst self to."

Franne is a master connector because she cherishes the value of being authentic in business and in life. As a result, she enjoys friendship and a booming business with clients who respect her style. By living the tenets of this secret, Franne says that she practices the cardinal rules for all relationships that I frequently preach.

Be True to Your Word

Franne says this rule has enabled her and her fifty-three-year-old partner to build trust over time by consistently being true to their word. They do what they say they are going to do. They are true to each other's word by respecting what is revealed through the explicit communication that they share about fears, dreams, expectations, happiness, and disappointment. And they are never afraid to express how they feel in the relationship. "Trust is not just a concept," Franne says. "It's a behavior, something that's demonstrated on a regular basis on an emotional, spiritual, mental, and physical level."

I practice what Franne McNeal preaches because it builds trust. For example, a friend of mine has often said, "George, I'll call you this afternoon." I have trusted that he would, but he routinely rings me back a week later! My friend is not promising what he can deliver. His failure to deliver on his promise was the same as when a printer told me, "George, I'll have your brochures finished on Monday." I believed her, but she didn't have them completed until Friday!

"Trust is not just a concept."

—business coach Franne McNeal

My response to these situations was that both people's lack of commitment to their spoken words eroded my trust. And without trust, our relationships weaken and dissolve. That's why it's imperative that you do what you say you're going to do. The book *The Four Agreements* by Don Miguel Ruiz says first and foremost: Be true to your word. People remember your words. So if you fail to do what you say you're going to do, you lose credibility. People will stop believing what you say. They won't trust you. And they won't want to depend on you to be their friend—or do business with you.

Use Your Voice to Add Value and Validate a Passionate Sense of Purpose and Strong Point of View

One of the most powerful tools in your personal press kit is your voice. It is the megaphone that you use to broadcast your authenticity to the world. Think about your voice. If you were blessed with a pleasant-sounding voice, then flaunt it—along with excellent grammar, diplomatic words, and a polite tone. Franne does this very well.

However, when I say voice, I'm not talking about the *sound* that comes out of your mouth. I'm talking about the *substance* of what you say. Each of us has a unique voice in the world—it is tuned by genetics, culture, health, our religious beliefs, and life experience. As a result, our voice—the messages and themes that we continually express to the world—could be one of harmony, discord, advocacy for the powerless, outrage against injustice, humor, and the list goes on.

My voice rings with the confidence of a man who rose from foster care, abuse, a broken family of eleven children, and a hardscrabble upbringing in Brooklyn, New York. I worked for years in dozens of frustrating jobs, and now I am fulfilling my life's passion and purpose as a speaker who uplifts and inspires people across America and the globe.

The voice I hear inside of me, and the wiring I was born with, have moved me in the direction of teaching people how to collaborate and value each other's diverse skills and unique purpose. I call this networking, connecting, and ultimately, clicking. It is crystal clear to me this is what I was born to do. Why? Because this is what I've always done in one way or another. This is what has blessed me with the greatest joy, fulfillment, and satisfaction. It is something I did naturally without pay for many years.

When the demand for me to speak on the themes that I am most passionate about became greater than the time I had available, I began charging for it, then writing about it, then building events, a conference, and a business to support my passion and the demand. At some point I was forced to make a critical decision: leave my job and dedicate my life to what I loved, or remain in the warm bosom of secure employment, familiar territory, and supportive friends. I chose to make a change, because I felt strongly about my belief.

In essence, I decided to free my authentic self so that it could evolve to its fullest potential. Had I stayed in the job that I did not enjoy, I would not have been true to myself. As President Franklin D. Roosevelt said, "The truth is found when men are free to pursue it." I freed myself to pursue my truth, my authentic self.

Had I not made the change, I would have been oppressing the real George Fraser for the sake of security. Ultimately, however, greater security than I ever imagined resulted from my leap of faith in becoming a full-time speaker. As I leaped, the security net did appear, but ever so slowly. Several times, I hit the net and bounced right back. It's been one hell of a free fall. When I speak on it, my voice rings with purpose and righteousness. It's infectious, contagious, and fulfilling.

Now, I want you to consider my quest to allow my voice to sing by freeing my authentic self. How can you do that to live your own dreams? Does your voice ring with enthusiasm as you talk about your true calling in life? Does your voice echo with the hope and excitement of your immigrant parents? Do you feel that your authentic self is motivated by your parents' prayers that you would achieve the glorious American Dream that was unfathomable in the nightmarish conditions they fled in their homeland? An example of this is the author Frank McCourt, who won the Pulitzer Prize for his book *Angela's Ashes* about his heart-wrenching roots in Ireland. Does your voice speak for a people once oppressed, now free to soar but still shackled by a hateful history? Dr. Martin Luther King Jr.'s voice literally and figuratively accomplished this in his famous 1963 "I have a dream" speech.

> *"The truth is found when men are free to pursue it."*
>
> —President Franklin D. Roosevelt

To help you analyze your own voice and assess how you can best put it to use, Stephen Covey, the author of *The 7 Habits of Highly Effective People*, has identified a way for you to find your voice and live a happier, more productive life. In *The 8th Habit: From Effectiveness to Greatness*, Covey breaks down our "voice" into four parts:

"Voice lies at the nexus of talent (your natural gifts and strengths), passion (those things that naturally energize, excite, motivate and inspire you), need (including what the world needs enough to pay you for) and conscience (that still small voice that assures you of what is right and that prompts you to actually do it)."

Covey says that finding your voice is your passport to your personal Promised Land. And there, you can showcase your talents and message in grand style. But don't promise to sing an opera when you've just signed up for singing lessons.

Know Your Limitations and Promise Only What You Can Deliver

This comes back to being real—with yourself. Sometimes in our excitement and enthusiasm to embark on a new adventure and opportunity, we overestimate our ability to do certain things. And despite our most energetic and well-meaning intentions, we're simply unrealistic.

The result? It backfires. When we cannot meet the deadline or produce all the product on time or downright fail, we look like a fraud. So take a moment to think about the things you say and the promises you make. Do you exaggerate? Does your exuberance about a new undertaking inspire you to underestimate the amount of time the work will require? Do you consistently fail to factor in obstacles and delays?

For example, is your new bakery business really ready to deliver that enormous order of two thousand cupcakes when you've never made more than five hundred at once? Can you really complete the report the same week that you have a business trip? There's a difference between stepping out on faith and jumping without a parachute. To avoid taking a plunge—and watching your reputation crash and burn—stop before you speak. Take a hard look at yourself, your capabilities, your time requirements. Then make an informed statement about what you can and cannot do. That way, you keep your reputation intact.

My reputation took a beating several years ago when I tried to give two keynote speeches on the same day, one in the morning and one that evening. That's possible if the venues are in close proximity, but these were not, one being north and the other southwest. Both of my friends who had booked me were dependent upon me being there. In fact their ticket sales were also dependent upon me being there.

But I did not keep it real. My superego won over my id. Your id, according to Freud, is preoccupied with a present perspective, or immediate gratification. Even though I'm an experienced traveler, I took this huge risk on double-booking myself in two cities in one day, knowing full well that anything could happen when traveling in the winter.

My worst nightmare came true. My flight to my second speech, in the southwest, was cancelled owing to weather conditions in the north. I couldn't get there under any circumstances, and I didn't finalize that conclusion until four hours before the engagement.

I was crushed and embarrassed. My host, Bob, was stuck without his "star attraction." It has never happened again, but every time I see my friend Bob, I apologize. I've even offered to waive my fee for a future engagement to make up for my mistake, but he hasn't taken me up on it. Someday he will forgive me. Hopefully, I'll get a chance to speak for him, and at that time I will apologize to him publicly for embarrassing him publicly. It is said that in life two things happen—you either win or you learn. If you don't learn at first, you will repeat the lesson until you do.

Never make a commitment you can't fully expect to keep, especially if it will seriously affect the public reputation of a friend. The trick to this is knowing yourself, backwards and forwards, and sticking with the truth. Then put your gifts and your passions on center stage, says the actor Laurence Fishburne. "I'm just being who I am," Fishburne says. "I don't dwell on it too much. I'm just a cat who has a gift and I've tried to nurture it and I've tried to choose carefully what I do and hopefully people will still dig it." He's an actor and he's just being real.

Be Yourself

Authentic people don't need you to lie to them to feed their egos. Authentic people live by their rules but don't expect you to follow them. Authentic people are at peace with themselves, so they don't have to prove anything to you.

I've heard a firefighter say that he's perfectly happy with his income and lifestyle, that he never feels the need for more money or more stuff. Instead, he appreciates the time that his flexible schedule allows him to enjoy with his family. I've also encountered people with advanced degrees who choose to take jobs such as delivering pizza or working in a restaurant. They are being authentic by doing what they enjoy. And they are disregarding the pressures of family, friends, and society that tell them they have to do more, earn more, get more. They are proof of Plato's words: "Truth is its own reward."

Many times when we're climbing to a certain stature in the business world—or perhaps we're there and we want to project sophistication—we take on a plastic, one-dimensional personality. We wear a mask of what we *think* we should be to show the world we're serious and ready to take charge.

But masks are stiff! Fake! Boring. They hide your wonderful personality. And they make people suspicious. That's the kiss of death to any relationship, because we must trust first. It's impossible to start a meaningful relationship from behind a façade. It comes off as if you're trying to hide something, and phoniness or extreme formality makes people uncomfortable.

"Truth is its own reward."

—Plato

But many men and women wear masks to hide a terrible truth about most people: that they suffer from low self-esteem and a lack of confidence. These are the number one afflictions of human beings, for a variety of reasons. They can be overcome, however, once we understand the cause.

Take, for example, a child who grows up as the third generation in a crime-ridden housing project, where his parents make racist remarks about his own race and tell him that their people never amount to anything. That child might internalize that negativity and think lowly of himself.

People who achieve greatness will always tell you that an aunt, an uncle, a teacher, a parent, a neighbor—someone who cared—took time to nurture their self-esteem to make them believe they could rise up and out of their circumstances. A child can succeed when someone tells him: "You are the child of the slaves who would not die. You have the DNA of the great kings and queens of Africa." A child's every life decision depends on how he feels about himself. When someone constantly reinforces his or her love for that child, the child can achieve greatness. Children are hardwired with high self-esteem. They inherently believe that they can do and become anything. But too often, other people beat them down.

So what's the difference between a low achiever and a multimillionaire who grew up in the same conditions? I call it a question of nature versus nurture. God hardwires some of us with the propensity to do right; He programs some of us with propensities to do wrong. The nurturing we get on top of this can make or break us.

My family is the perfect example. I am one of eleven children. My mother was married twice and had five children when she met my dad; she was institutionalized when I was young. My father drove a cab to support his six children with Mom, but it became too much. We were put into an orphanage first, then split up into foster homes around the toughest parts of New York City. Dad remained connected to his biological and stepchildren as well as his wife; he never remarried and worked hard to keep us connected.

I studied and stayed out of trouble, even though we lived in a rough neighborhood. The schools were mediocre, but I graduated, spent a few semesters in college, then finally got a good job with Procter & Gamble, married, had two sons, and ultimately found my purpose and my passion as an entrepreneur and motivational speaker. My older sister Emma and younger brother Joseph, with whom I grew up, had different stories. Emma found her passion in teaching, earned four degrees—one from Harvard—and went on to become assistant superintendent of a suburban New York school system before retiring after thirty-five years of service.

My younger brother Joseph, however, was always in trouble. He ran the streets, did poorly in school, and sold drugs. He was killed, along with two friends, during a drug deal that went bad.

My brother is dead, I'm living a purposeful, prosperous life, and Emma graduated from Harvard. Even though we had the same strict discipline and work ethic instilled in us by our foster parents, how did Joseph's life end up so different from Emma's and mine?

The difference was his choice of friends, the relationships he selected to impress with a false sense of toughness that was not really him. It is the same reason for their misfortune that I hear today from 95 percent of the men in prisons where I speak.

I believed my inner voice when it said I could do and be anything if I stayed in school, remained true to being myself, stayed out of trouble, and picked the right friends. My brother heard a different voice and chose different role models and followed different friends. I chose friends who shared my beliefs and who were achieving at a higher level than I was. My brother chose friends who shared his beliefs, and his two best friends were also killed with him. We choose our relationships; they can

If you are the smartest person in your network, you're in the wrong network.

raise us up or drag us down. If you are the smartest person in your network, you're in the wrong network.

This applies to the business world as well. We choose to cultivate and nurture our relationships to increase our opportunity to add value and get a good exchange. The more people to whom you can serve and add value, the greater you will be enriched. And the simplest way you can do that is by showing love and appreciation. We all want to be loved and appreciated, and we can do that for each other with simple words. Show people that you care, that you believe in them, and they will blossom.

Good manners reflect a well-ordered person. I believe that "excuse me," "thank you," and "please" are the three great lubricants of life; use them generously and they will solve 95 percent of your problems. Manners are part of being real and yanking off the phony masks. What are other ways to be real?

The more people to whom you can serve and add value, the greater you will be enriched.

Get in touch with the real you by becoming aware of yourself when you're relaxed. The next time you're enjoying a mellow evening with friends, pay attention to your body. You'll notice that your muscles are loose, your face is relaxed, and you speak in an animated way, saying humorous things.

Next, compare those sensations to your stiff, self-conscious posture at a formal business meeting or in an uncomfortable social situation. Study how you feel. Are your eyebrows scrunched in a super-serious scowl? Are your muscles tense? Are you speaking in an unnatural, formal cadence?

Now, how can you bring the natural you—the ones your friends adore—to every situation, no matter how formal? By envisioning the natural you in a business setting or a formal social event. Think about how relaxed you would like to feel, talk, and move—free of fear, self-scrutiny, and falsities about how you "think" you're "sup-posed" to act. See yourself this way in your mind's eye as you walk into the crowded meeting room or into a restaurant to meet a new client.

Show people that you care, that you believe in them, and they will blossom.

Of course, always be appropriate. Loosening up does not mean being offensive, crass, or obnoxious. Main-tain good manners and etiquette. Just let your personality bust out of the mask and stiff body language. Relax. Enjoy. Be yourself. Keep it real. And be consistent; don't fabricate what you think is the natural you. Because time will tell. Consis-tency confirms authenticity!

Create an Air of Distinction and Build the Brand Called You, Inc.

The way you present yourself physically is very important. It's part of your personal press kit that reflects the real you: letterheads, business cards, office space, your hairstyle, your grooming, your clothes. Like it or not, looks matter. We are judged every day by how we look. Design and taste matter a lot. In fact, a recent study proved that women who wore makeup got better service in stores than cosmetic-free women. And I guarantee: walk into any restau-rant or store in a business suit, and the staff will be more attentive and accommodating than if you're wearing jeans, a T-shirt, and a baseball cap.

In these days of casual attire in the workplace, the line between the dos and don'ts of what's appropriate has been blurred. My advice? Always err on the side of caution—overdressing is always better than underdressing. You never know whom you'll meet, and you want to always be presentable, whether you're dealing with the copy machine repair technician or the CEO. As the British clergy-man and author Thomas Fuller said, "Good clothes open all doors." I also love what the Greek philosopher Epictetus said: "Know first who you are; and then adorn yourself accordingly."

If you are easy on the eyes, that's a gift from God—use it. But beauty is in the eye of the beholder and everyone, regardless of their features or size, can enhance or screw up whatever God has given them. Oprah Winfrey was not a natural beauty, but she worked hard on her persona and look. After going through several different looks, her size, hair, makeup, and wardrobe found just the right natural combination to complement her dynamic and charismatic personality. Today, many TV personalities attempt to imitate Oprah's distinct style and point of view.

Ed Brown writes in *10 Plus Ways to Gain Recognition Within Your Profession,* "If we were to dissect two human beings, there would be little difference in the physical composition of each. The major com-ponents that make humans different are their modes of thinking and expression. Consequently, your view-point about the world and your role in it are often conveyed in your self expression. The car you drive, clothes that you wear and your style of communications—verbally and non-verbally illustrate your degree of distinction."

Dr. Kwa David Whitaker is a Ph.D. in psychology, a practic-ing attorney, and the founder of four African-centered charter schools in the hardcore urban centers of Cleveland, Akron, and Youngstown, Ohio. I serve as his board chair for each of the schools. His passion about the need to immerse and center black children in their African history as part of the building of their self-esteem and self-confidence is evident not only in his superior interper-sonal speaking and writing skills, but also in his name, demeanor, sense of humor, and attire.

"Kwa" is Ghanaian for "born on Thursday." His brilliance, wis-dom, easygoing personality, and soft-spokenness make you com-fortable in his presence. And his African attire makes him distinctive. It is not off-putting in any business or social setting; it is not an outlandish costume he wears. It makes a statement of his purpose, his life's work, and his voice, and therefore has a positive and influential impact on his various audiences.

My look is more traditional, classic business attire. In that way I'm still "old school," but it works for me. I wear "power colors," dark pinstriped suits, and two-tone shirts with French cuffs. I add a little flair with expensive but classic shoes and bold ties knotted with a dimple. I wear no jewelry except my watch. I like the look of Ralph Lauren, the investment banker Vernon Jordan, and TV personality Charlie Rose of PBS.

Why? I see myself as a leader and successful businessman. I passionately speak and write on economic development, wealth creation, and the power and importance of relationships. I believe first impressions are critical, and they reflect one's point of view and purpose. Although I don't go on the golf course dressed that way (I do, however, consider myself to be a well-groomed golfer), when I show up to do my work I want to stand out, to look, smell, and feel successful. Yes, I want to create an air of distinction, and it's easily done when you know who you really are. I share all of this about myself to show that I am authentic. I am being true to the essence of George Fraser in the way I think, act, speak, dress, nurture relationships, and do business. I know that everybody appreciates a person who gives his or her best. And I know that I cannot fix others before first fixing myself.

> *I cannot fix others before first fixing myself.*

"Regardless of age, regardless of position, regardless of the business we happen to earn, all of us need to understand the importance of branding. We are the CEO's of our own companies: Me, Inc. To be in business today, our most important job is to be head marketer of the brand called you," says longtime business guru Tom Peters.

We get only one act on this stage of life. If you want the standing ovation—in the form of fulfillment, wealth, and the chance to make your gifts light up other people's lives—then take center stage and give 'em all you've got—before the show is over and the curtain falls. Do it with a smile and style, make them laugh, and do it with all your heart . . . Click.

Exercise for Truth #1

If you're not real with yourself, you can't make genuine connections with others. So take the time now to evaluate how you can be more authentic.

1. You are the CEO of You, Inc. Take an audit of every department to evaluate which are working at optimum productivity and which need improvement.

   Personality:
   Speech:
   Dress:
   Health:
   Greetings:
   Cordiality:
   Moods:

2. We all hold illusions about ourselves. But if the illusion clashes with reality, you can make a phony impression, which is a turn-off. What illusions do you hold about yourself? How realistic are they? And how can you cast off the illusions to become more real?

3. Do you exaggerate? Stretching the truth for the sake of a grandiose story boils down to lying. Get real with yourself about

why you exaggerate. And focus on ways that you can stick to the truth the next time you're telling a story or making a business proposal.

4. Ask a friend to give you an honest critique of how you come across in social and professional situations. Are you stiff? Relaxed? Personable? Aloof? Based on their comments, brainstorm how you can cultivate a warmer, more genuine aura that increases your chances to click with new people.

Key **CLICK** Factors

Always
- Do what you say you're going to do and promise only what you can deliver.

Keep in Mind
- Fix yourself first, and then help fix others. You can't give what you don't have, and you can't teach what you don't know.

Do Not
- Act, speak, or live the way you think you "should" according to what your friends and family want.
- Ignore your inner voice that tells you how to think, speak, and live in a way that's true to yourself.

Make Sure To
- Build a distinct and unique brand that is credible, trustworthy, and compelling.

Communicate with Your Heart

When your heart speaks, take good notes.

—Unknown

THE BEST CONNECTIONS are rooted in the synergy of great communication. When you listen with and speak from your heart, you enhance your words with a sense of humor, empathy, compassion, and a smile.

Heart Dynamics 101

The research on the function of the heart clearly shows that the heart can play an important role in facilitating positive changes in attitude and emotional well-being. According to Doc Childre and Deborah Rozman in their book *Transforming Stress*, "The

heart is both a physical organ and an intuitive feeling center . . .
The heart is a source of intelligence." The field of neurocardiology
has shown the link between the heart
and the brain. The brain and the heart
are interconnected, and emotions are
transmitted to the brain via pathways
from the heart.

The best connections are

rooted in the synergy of great

communication.

What we now know is that communicating from the heart is not just an
expression. The heart has a brain, and
we control that brain through our thoughts. Think positively, and
you are on the road to building the skills necessary to become a
great communicator. Therefore, speaking from the heart is not
rooted in sentimentality, as so often thought, but grounded in scientific research that clearly validates the heart-brain connection
and its role in enhancing communication.

Research affirms that the heart plays a vital role in transmitting
messages to the brain regarding the emotional state of an individual. When you are upset, the heart lets the brain know this, and
coherence is affected. In other words—you cannot think clearly!
If you can't think, then you can't communicate effectively. On
the other hand, when feelings of well-being exist, your problem-
solving abilities are enhanced. These enhanced abilities create the
synergy and chemistry that facilitate greater communication, which
enhances the Click factor between individuals and even groups.

The process of utilizing the heart to create positive emotional
synergy represents a major breakthrough into the understanding
of the heart's vital role as a thinking organ with a mind of its own.
In essence, the heart is not just a pump but an organ that works in
collaboration with the brain to regulate the emotional landscape of
the body. As reported in *The Coherent Heart* (McCraty, Atkinson,
Tomasino, and Bailey 2005), neurocardiologists have confirmed

that our emotions affect our ability to think coherently. When we are upset or frustrated, clarity and thought patterns are negatively affected. However, when we are in control of our emotions, there is a definite increase in our ability to think intelligently about a situation. In other words, you cannot maximize your brain power when you are out of sync—chemistry is off, synergy is interrupted, and communication suffers. When you are in a state of appreciation, you maximize your brain power.

As a result, when you are a positive poised individual in control of your emotions, you are more readily approachable and invite conversation, and others are drawn to you. Everyone benefits when you speak from the heart. Your facial expressions, your eyes (the windows of the soul), and your body language align, sending a clear message that you are in communication mode. Tuning into your positive heart energy is vital to expressive language that captures the sincerity of the words being spoken.

Speak from Your Heart

Rachelle Franklin is proof that a simple phone call in the name of networking can blossom into a rich and rare connection with a cherished friend and mentor. Ever since she introduced me fifteen years ago when I gave a speech at her company, Motorola, Rachelle and I have enjoyed many thought-provoking conversations.

A master networker with the business acumen to match, Rachelle has successfully navigated the treacherous political waters of the corporate executive suite and the complex multitask duties of a wife (of a nonprofit organization executive), a mom (three children), a dog lover, and a suburban homemaker in an upscale Florida community. This petite Southern charmer with looks to match knows all the right questions to ask. Her razor sharp inquiries are seasoned with humor and accented with a smile. She listens for the words not spoken—the real meaning of what is said. Her response always adds value and contributes, but doesn't dominate the conversation.

After our initial networking contact at her company, Rachelle and I connected quickly based on common ground and interests. As she climbed the corporate ladder, she traveled around the world. We lost contact for a while but were reconnected by a mutual friend during Rachelle's short stint as vice president of integrated brand marketing for Office Depot. It was then that chemistry, fit, and timing aligned perfectly for us.

We clicked. And we've been involved in each other's business, careers, and lives ever since. We both know that whatever we have at our disposal that may help one another, access is just a phone chat away. During our chats, she has shared with me the fascinating way in which she connected with her friend and mentor.

It happened two decades ago, when Rachelle was one of the few minority female executives in a Fortune 50 company. At the time, her employer hired another black woman who was touted as one of the best marketers in America because she had introduced the first black Barbie doll for Mattel.

Rachelle initiated a life-changing communication by calling the woman, who worked in the company's Chicago offices. In hindsight, Rachelle says she was motivated to call by her lifelong endorsement of Truth #7: Tailor Your Relationships for the Perfect Fit—treat others as they wish to be treated. And every new employee wants to be treated with a warm welcome.

"I picked up the phone and said from the heart, 'Hi, I'm Rachelle Franklin. I work in the Florida offices; welcome to the company. If there's anything I can do for you, let me know.' It was very superficial networking. But nothing starts with connecting. It starts with networking." However, Rachelle says she felt an immediate chemistry over the phone with Jocelyn.

"During the phone conversation, I felt like I knew her," Rachelle says. "At the core of our connection was probably the fact that we were two black females in a very white, male-dominated, technical environment." Their conversation was so unique and special that it inspired Rachelle to pamper the relationship by keeping in touch. Then Jocelyn was transferred to the company's Florida offices for an international assignment.

"Life is funny with its twists and turns," Rachelle says, adding that she again offered to help Jocelyn with her new position. "I took it a step further and I invited her and her family over for dinner. I looked at it like Truth #3: Love, Serve, Give, and Add Value—First!"

Rachelle says that by opening her home and her heart to her colleague, she immediately knew they were destined for more than a casual work relationship. They socialized regularly, and Rachelle invited Jocelyn to join monthly events with a group of black professional women. At the time, Rachelle and her husband were starting their family of three children. Since Jocelyn had older children, she shared mother-wit with Rachelle, which deepened their rapport and bond.

Another important dynamic was playing out to mark this as the type of extraordinary connection that Daniel Goleman writes about in his book *Social Intelligence: The New Science of Human Relationships*. Psychologist Robert Rosenthal (formerly at Harvard, now at the University of California, Riverside) says, based on his landmark study "The Nature of Rapport," that when two people click, their chemistry must contain three elements: "mutual attention, shared positive feeling, and a well-coordinated nonverbal duet."

The result? The foundation for the kind of enduring relationship that Rachelle and Jocelyn enjoy today. In fact, their bond epitomizes the characteristics of great relationships that Rosenthal observed in his study. Rosenthal put people in pairs, then asked one person to wear a bandage over a painful-looking splinter. That expression "I feel your pain," literally played out if the two people were clicking. How? The researcher observed that if the bandaged person grimaced, his partner winced as well. No surprise—partners who were not clicking were oblivious to the other person's pain.

In addition, Rosenthal's study confirmed another important dynamic that manifested for Rachelle and Jocelyn—nonverbal cues such as happy and attentive facial expressions, welcoming body language, and a pleasant tone of voice. Their exchanges also epitomized how eye contact, physical closeness, and comfortable silences help cement the bond that's formed when two people click.

Though Rachelle and Jocelyn were not part of Rosenthal's study, the study sheds scientific light on the extraordinary nature of their relationship. And their bond deepened even more when the company announced that Rachelle's job would be transferred to Chicago. "I did not want to move to Chicago. I wanted to stay in my field of expertise, marketing and communication," she said. Plus, her husband, Patrick, had a great job, their children were in school, and they loved their lifestyle in upscale, oceanfront Boca Raton.

So Rachelle consulted with Jocelyn about her dilemma. And Jocelyn listened aggressively, showing empathy and concern, seeking first to understand the situation, then to understand how she could help. She also listened to Rachelle's feelings, not just her ideas. In addition, Jocelyn considered the "change indicators" in Rachelle's life—with a family and a wonderful lifestyle, Rachelle was not willing to sacrifice her personal success for a new professional commitment. With that, Jocelyn tailored a solution to Rachelle's dilemma that perfectly suited Rachelle's lifestyle and desires, both personally and professionally.

Rachelle recalls: "Jocelyn looked in her own world of opportunity and said, 'I have an opportunity for you.'" Suddenly, a mentor/mentee relationship evolved. Jocelyn arranged for Rachelle to work for her in South Florida in a position that was quite different from anything Rachelle had done. "It was a life-changing decision," Rachelle says. "I went out of my comfort zone and did something that I wasn't an expert at doing every day. What started as a role in organizational design—helping the company to build its consumer marketing talent base—led to the ultimate marketing job of doing branding for the company on a global basis."

Then Jocelyn moved to a position at another thriving company. She eventually invited Rachelle to join her there. Today, many years since that first phone call, the relationship continues to deepen and evolve. Rachelle is a global marketing consultant, while Jocelyn runs charter schools that she founded with her husband, Edward.

"We meet regularly, and we talk about what we want to do with our lives. Our relationship speaks to the power of networking and the power of connecting. We exemplify how going through all Ten Truths gets you to an extraordinary relationship . . . a click."

What allowed Rachelle to immediately click with Jocelyn? The chemistry, fit, and timing of their relationship aligned perfectly. First, the "chemistry" was right because they shared that intangible gut feeling, or vibe, that they were like-minded and compatible. As for "fit," they shared the unique position at the time of being African American women in prominent positions in corporate America. And the "timing" was just right because they felt the need for companionship—both by phone and when they lived nearby in Florida.

Another Truth to their extraordinary relationship? Exquisite communication skills. "When we sit down," Rachelle says, "it's an exchange. If the mentor is doing all of the talking, something is wrong. If you are in a mentor/mentee relationship, you have to listen with real intention. You'll hear more of what their heart is saying. If they're speaking from the heart, then you communicate back, 'This is what I think I'm hearing you say.' "

Speaking from the heart, as opposed to saying what you think the other person wants to hear, is rooted in something that Jocelyn advises all the time: "You have to know what you want." Rachelle says that every time she ponders a decision, her thoughts echo with that command spoken with her mentor's voice. Rachelle adds that you cannot *get* what you want out of life until you *know* what you want. And people cannot help you acquire what you want if you don't even know. "A lot of people want others to tell them what they should do or what options they're going to put on the table for them."

Rachelle says in addition to heeding her mentor's advice about knowing what she wants, she applies that idea to her eighteen-year marriage. Recently, as Rachelle contemplated a move to Texas to live closer to her aging parents, Jocelyn warned, "Whatever you do, just make sure that you and your husband are doing it together. Together. Don't make decisions based on you. When you make these big life changes, make sure you're moving in lockstep."

Jocelyn can successfully offer valid advice because she understands the keys to Rachelle's heart: a strong marriage, a happy home life, and personal happiness. Jocelyn is also a wonderful friend because she appreciates that over time, our priorities and desires change, so we must tailor our friendship and advice to those changes.

Rachelle says the heartfelt communication that she enjoys with Jocelyn exemplifies the power of the Ten Truths in this book.

"No one person takes you through the journey of life," Rachelle says. "It's a myriad of relationships and experiences that help you through."

How can you improve your communication skills so that you can enjoy the type of deep connection that Rachelle shares with Jocelyn?

Learn to Express Your Feelings and Ideas in an Instant

We are not responsible for all the stuff that comes into our minds, but we are responsible for the things that come out of our mouths. Start thinking about your words—what you say, how you say them, and how you write them. Because your ability to connect with people starts with a first impression, and our speaking and writing can either enhance or ruin that impression.

Have you ever met someone who's impeccably groomed and dressed, but they speak gibberish with bad grammar and profanity? Poor communication skills tarnish our impressions of people. Here are several techniques for making sure that you are presenting the most polished person possible.

To start, tape record yourself. Just as athletes critique their performance by watching their games on videotape, you can tape record your conversations while chatting with a friend, your spouse, or your children. Giving a lecture to the board of directors or at your church? Set the recorder on the podium and get it all on tape. Then, analyze it. As you lis-

We are not responsible for all the stuff that comes into our minds, but we are responsible for the things that come out of our mouths.

ten, pinpoint obvious flaws such as the "um" affliction or repetitive filler phrases such as "you know what I mean?" Does your voice rise at the end of a sentence like you're asking a question when you're making a statement? If so, make a conscious effort to stop doing that; it makes you sound unsure of yourself, as if you're asking permission. Instead, speak with confidence and authority.

Also, budget your words. "Always say less than necessary," writes Robert Greene in his book, *The 48 Laws of Power*. When you say as much as possible with as few words as possible, you give more power to each word. Too many folks bombard us with meaningless *over-explain-itis*. They expound on boring, irrelevant details that waste everyone's time.

So don't tell your boss: "I couldn't finish the report in time because the ink cartridge on the printer ran out and I had to dash to the storeroom to get another, but they were out, too, so I had to go down to the third floor to see if Shari in marketing had one and luckily she did but by the time I got back . . ."

Blah, blah, blah. Your boss does not want to hear all that. Instead, say: "The report will be ready at five. We had a technical snag; I apologize for the delay. It will be perfect." Then next time, make sure your printer is stocked with ink well before your report is due.

Meanwhile, as you critique your tape-recorded presentation, ask for help from an expert. Any friend or associate who speaks and writes well and is a great listener can pinpoint grammatical errors, repetition, monotone speech patterns, slang, and negativity. By negativity I mean expressions such as: "I could drop dead from all this pressure; this project is horrible!"; or self-criticism like, "I'm such a loser, always doing the drudge-work around here"; or whining, "I hate it when the cafeteria serves beef Stroganoff"; or put-downs such as, "We peons never get any respect," or, "I'm broke, as usual."

Words have incredible power, so speak what you want in positive terms: "I'm giving this project 200 percent effort. It will succeed!" and "Fortunately, the delivery van was late so I had extra time to make some phone calls," and "Let's all check out that lunchtime jazz in the park when the cafeteria serves beef Stroganoff," and "I'm strategizing how to earn my fortune."

Training oneself to dwell on positive ideas and expressions is just as important as curing oneself of an all-too-pervasive attention-deficit disorder that I believe is induced by our high-tech lifestyles. With cell phones ringing, pagers vibrating, computer screens flashing, and everything moving at laser speed, it seems that we have all lost the ability to patiently sit still and focus. Our overstimulated lives make it difficult to listen—and get others to listen to us. Even our news is delivered in short snippets and sound bites about what's happening in our world.

We are overwhelmed by endless demands. Everyone has limited time and energy. Most people you'd like to reach can't spare a moment; they're booked and overloaded. So if you want to get their attention, you'd better grab it wherever you are.

Make Instant Impressions

Whether right or wrong, this is the reality of the world in which we are living, loving, and doing business. As a result, we must learn to make instant impressions so that we can connect and click in personal and professional situations. Therefore, when a split-second opportunity presents itself, you must express yourself quickly, clearly, compellingly, and memorably.

The best way to do this is to create an engaging *sound bite*—a descriptive message that you can deliver in less than fifteen seconds when you meet new people. Your personal sound bite should capture your listeners' attention with information that stimulates their appetite for more.

Make your sound bite interesting. It should attract immediate *attention*, and it should be memorable and powerful enough to stir overloaded listeners into action. In fifteen to twenty seconds, your sound bite must explain:

- Who you are
- Where you're from
- What you do
- How you add value and/or make a difference
- A quantitative analysis of your added value

Here's my sound bite: "Hi, I'm George Fraser from Cleveland, Ohio, by way of Brooklyn, New York. I'm the founder of FraserNet, Inc. I put on networking events, write books, and speak on connecting and building effective relationships. I can help you turn acquaintances into friends, and your contacts into contracts. Over the last twenty years I've helped over two thousand people find the right job and/or secure over $500 million in new business." It's seventy-one words long, covers all the key bases, and takes less than twenty seconds to say. If I pique someone's interest, they will invite me to tell them more.

This is my method for speaking my way into phenomenal relationships. You can do this, too. And if you feel the need to improve your speaking skills, you can get professional help by joining a group like Toastmasters International. At regular meetings, these folks gather for the purpose of improving their public speaking skills. You don't have to become a public speaker—but you will be able to effectively express yourself in any situation: to tell your doctor exactly what ails you; to succinctly inform your boss of the status of the project; and to convince clients how they can benefit from your products and services. You will become a better communicator to your spouse, your children, and the world. And that will connect you in deep, rewarding relationships.

In "The Act of Speaking with Flair," one of the best articles I've read on the subject of public speaking, Ed Brown of the Core Edge Image and Charisma Institute explains several key ways to communicate so that you make a spectacular and unforgettable impression.

First, Brown recommends that you study speakers who grab and keep your attention. Figure out why they captivate you. Is it their tone of voice? Body language? Their clever and powerful use of words, phrases, and anecdotes?

Then Brown encourages you to emulate that style. Reinvent yourself by incorporating those bedazzling techniques into your own conversations and presentations. At the same time, brand your speaking style with key words and phrases that are unique to you and your message. Hopefully, as a result, your audiences will be awestruck and inspired.

As you train yourself to master the art of communication, always be conscious of two things that researchers say can make or break a "click moment": body language and tone of voice. You get one chance to make a first impression, and once it's done, you can't push a delete button to start over. So what's the best way to critique your communication style?

Interrogate Your Friends

"Interrogate your friends," Proverbs 1:5 advises us. Every one of us is a rich well of knowledge; we should immerse our buckets every day and drink in the abundance.

You can do this with the help of your friends, says Theodore Zeldin, author of the book *Conversation: How Talk Can Change Our Lives*. He advocates sparking "conversations for action" by asking your friends to have a conversation about you to reveal insights that you can use to transform yourself into a charismatic communicator. You can also do this by "interviewing" the three most successful people you know well. Muster up the courage and curiosity to pose those burning questions, and you may learn nuggets of wisdom that boost you into a new realm of success.

> *Every one of us is a rich well of knowledge; we should immerse our buckets every day and drink in the abundance.*

I find that all the knowledge I need is patiently awaiting my discovery inside the minds of my friends and associates. But it's my job to pose the questions to retrieve those life-changing insights. Believe me, I'm never shy! Almost daily, I embark on a journalistic quest for answers that propel me onward and upward in personal and professional relationships.

Take It to the Next Level: Writing

Once you're comfortable and confident with your speaking, get ready to catapult your communication onward and upward—by writing. Written words can be even more powerful than spoken words because they can remain forever. So, hone your writing skills. If you're self-conscious about your writing, don't be. I'm not saying everybody can become a Shakespeare or a Stephen King or a J. K. Rowling or a Maya Angelou. But do the best with what you have.

◆ **Assess your skills.** Analyze the strengths and weaknesses of your writing by asking someone you trust, someone with excellent writing skills, to critique your writing. If you're a nurse, show that person samples of your patients' reports. If you're a barbershop owner, show them the ad that you wrote. If you have an e-business, show them text from your website. Then, if you have grammar issues, or if you need to work on making your writing flow smoothly, you'll know where to start. Then:

◆ **Take a class.** Attend a writing conference, a community college course, or an on-the-job-writing workshop. Consider the time and money as a crucial investment in your success.

　What you write today in your journal, on your job, or even in a book, will immortalize you. Hundreds of years from now, people may enjoy the pleasure of reading the ideas that popped into your brain. That's power!

◆ **Practice makes perfect.** Writing is just like exercising: the more you do it, the stronger you become. So write in a journal; the therapeutic value of this is worth the time and effort alone.

　You can also practice by writing old-fashioned letters. Use flair and creativity as you compose e-mails, thank-you notes, letters—and anything else you "have" to write for work. Remember, most successful people are bombarded by spoken and written words every day. Make yours jump up off the page and dance! That will enchant people and endear them to you in both professional and personal relationships.

◆ **Read!** Yes, use your eyes to learn how to write with your hands. Something in that brilliant machine inside our heads has a mechanism that transforms reading into better writing. Call it osmosis, but studies show that the more you read, the better writer you become.

And while reading is a silent act, so is the next step toward becoming a master communicator and connector:

♦ **Write with authority.** At every opportunity, you should position yourself as an expert within your profession. Low-cost newsletters and website directives on published articles can do more with less investment than a full-blown advertising campaign. People are looking for someone they can trust; make that someone be you through your authoritative command of words.

Develop Good Listening Skills

In our turbocharged, impatient world that bombards us with noise and movement, the art of listening gets blasted as we dash up the road to achievement. But too often we go through the motions of listening, not hearing a word. Here's an example. I was recently walking through an office when a young man said:

"Hey George, how ya doin' today?"

"I've got the flu and I lost my wallet," I answered.

"Great, loved your speech the other day," the guy said. He was not listening or connecting. He just kept walking.

But if I'm a great connector, my job is to get you talking about you. For example, when two master networkers are talking to each other, you'll hear one say, "Enough about me. Let's talk about you." They're always reversing the conversation. My advice: Don't talk about yourself. Of course, as I said earlier, you should give enough information so that people know who you are and what you do. Always be ready to roll tape on your sixty-second commercial for You, Inc. Make it captivating and concise, and then close your mouth, open your ears, and . . . Listen.

Good listeners are sincerely interested in you, and that makes you feel important. Because they're available for honest and genuine discussion, good listeners make you want to share yourself.

Bill Richardson, a former UN ambassador, credits his great listening skills with a coup for his career—and the world. How? By listening carefully, he discovered that former Iraqi Deputy Prime Minister Tariq Aziz was a Chaldean Catholic. Being Catholic himself, Richardson invited Aziz to attend church with him. During that intimate religious experience, they clicked so powerfully that Richardson was able to successfully negotiate for the release of two Americans by Saddam Hussein.

Just as Mr. Richardson found a way for Mr. Aziz to listen to him, my friend Dr. Joel Freeman says he makes an effort to cultivate his listening skills with his wife. "Sometimes I condense and repeat what she's saying to show that I heard her and processed what she was saying. I am by no means the world's best listener and my wife will tell you, I still struggle. I'm trying very hard to be present with her."

He says he responds to her statements about her day as a teacher, for example, by asking questions about a specific student with whom she's had a previous struggle. "That shows I've been listening to past conversations and not looking at the TV or playing with my laptop. I turn off the TV and the cell phone when she's talking to let her know she has top priority."

As Joel knows, listening teaches us and guides us along the wisest path. That's why I've devised some tricks to listening and learning as you talk and connect with people.

◆ **Be curious and real.** I am motivated by the pleasure of learning. If you are not interested in people or learning but want to connect with people, then start with a compliment and a question: "Hey, Sarah, great article you wrote in the company newsletter. How'd you learn to write like that?" Or "Mr. Jones, your testimonial in church was very touching. What's your secret to getting through tragedy without letting anger get the best of you?"

Or quite simply, "Hi, Mary. How are you today, really?" That last word, spoken with concern, lets her know I really care. That pushes an OPEN UP button inside her to reply with sincerity.

Successful people ask better questions. As a result, they get better answers. If your questions sound phony or motivated by greed or jealousy, the other person will feel that vibe and clam up. So be real, or don't bother.

◆ **Make sure your listener is truly listening.** If you think you're facing a "fake listener"—someone who nods with a blank expression and says, "that's interesting"—call them out. Say, "What specifically do you think is interesting?" And if their body language screams "not listening"—lack of eye contact, foot tapping, fidgety hands, or slumping posture— then say, "You've hardly spoken. Does that mean you support or object to this plan?"

> *"Quality questions create a quality life."*
>
> —Anthony Robbins

◆ **Focus.** Give them a minute, and some folks will ramble from here to eternity. If you let them. The trick is to rein in the conversation when it begins to drift: "Let's get back to that terrifying moment you were sharing about the poisonous jellyfish on your deep sea dive." Also, watch *The Oprah Winfrey Show.* Oprah's master interviewing skills enable her to slice a person off, mid-sentence, to sculpt the conversation her way. Yet she does it with such finesse, you hardly notice she's doing what would be rude for others: interrupting someone as they talk. Watch her, learn, and emulate her precision.

Here are other ways to ease someone into conversation:

♦ **Get them in your shoes.** Sometimes, if I'm dressed in a pin-striped suit and I've just lit up an auditorium with a speech, it's important for me to shrink that larger-than-life aura before I can mingle with people in the audience. I can only connect with them if we are standing on common ground so that they feel comfortable chatting, getting autographed books, and asking for advice. How do I achieve this? I put people in my shoes by saying something like: "Boy, am I starved. Know where I can get a good Rueben around here?"

And once we begin talking, the best way to get someone to open up is to:

♦ **Avoid yes and no questions.** Instead, ask questions that begin with who, what, when, where, how, and why. "Why" questions are especially effective. Like a three-year-old who's just discovered the word *why*, those three letters can bless you with access to hours of the most titillating secrets.

♦ **Go with your gut.** If the chemistry is flat and the conversation feels like you're trying to make ice cream from lemons, then politely move on. If the person you need to talk to is in a bad mood, dare to butter them up. Larry King does it. He says when Raquel Welch came to his show with a bad attitude, he gave her a hug. She calmed down. When world boxing champ Mike Tyson showed up brooding, King playfully asked, "Aww, is Mikey angry today? What's bothering Mikey?" The boxer laughed. King says he's taking a risk, but when he follows his instincts, they always guide him into the best interviews.

Great connectors like Larry King and Oprah Winfrey share a subtle ability to convey to their subjects love, serving, giving, and adding value to the conversation. Because of that, they tend to open people up and get the most out of them . . . Click.

Exercise for Truth #2

We're all guilty of saying what we think someone wants to hear. We do this with our friends, our spouses, and our business associates. Sometimes it feels like going along is just the way to get along. But that's not the best way to click in business or in life, because when we speak false words, they often come back to haunt us. Try this exercise.

1. Think of three instances where you've said what you think someone else wants to hear, just for the sake of keeping the peace, the business deal, or the friendship.

   A.
   B.
   C.

   Now think of three ways that you could have spoken the truth, from your heart and soul, in a way that would have preserved the peace, the business deal, or the friendship.

A.

B.

C.

Commit to yourself that you will resist the temptation to hold back and instead honestly speak your mind. Tell yourself, "I have the courage to speak my mind." Be purposeful and not hurtful. Honesty is the best policy only when it is purposeful. A lot of people speak in the name of honesty and wound somebody. If being honest is going to wound someone, don't be honest.

2. Are you an excellent listener? Or are you constantly waiting for the other person to finish speaking so that you can talk? Communicating from the heart means giving people undivided attention. So, for the next three conversations that you have:

   A. Focus entirely on the speaker. Turn off your cell phone. Look him in the eye. Repeat back to her what she is saying. And process his words so that you can respond with a thoughtful question that shows your genuine interest.

   B. Catch yourself when you're tempted to interrupt. Literally bite down if necessary. And think of how frustrated you feel when people cut you off while you're speaking.

   C. After the conversation, take mental notes of or even write on a business card or in a notebook some of the information that you gleaned. Refer back to those notes before speaking with this person the next time; he or she will be delighted that you remembered the details of your previous conversation.

Key **CLICK** Factors

Always
- Listen intently.
- Focus on the person.
- Be in the moment—as if there's nothing more important at that moment than what that person is saying.
- Seek first to understand, then to be understood.
- Keep the other person in mind. It's not about you; it's about the people around you.
- Make them feel important. Everybody wants to be significant and to be recognized.

Keep in Mind
- It's not about you. It's about the people around you. Many people are so concerned about themselves and the impressions they are making that they lose their naturalness and spontaneity and thus a chance to enhance the chemistry of the connection.

Do Not
- Criticize another person's dream. Instead, reaffirm their lofty vision and their pursuit to realize it. Ask good questions, and give encouragement and a helping hand wherever you can.

Make Sure To
- Recognize a person's importance and thereby make him or her feel important. Every person's deepest lifelong desire is to be significant and to be recognized.

Love, Serve, Give, and Add Value—First!

If you want happiness for an hour—take a nap

If you want happiness for a day—go fishing

If you want happiness for a month—get married

If you want happiness for a year—inherit a fortune

If you want happiness for a lifetime—help others

—Chinese Proverb

OUR PURPOSE IN life is to love, to serve, to give, and to add value to someone or something. With that in mind, you should enter every relationship by asking: How do I add value? How can I use my talents, connections, and resources to enhance this person's business and life? This is a biblical truth—to get, we must give first. That is, the best way to help *me* is to help *you*. It's as easy as giving a compliment. When you do and say something nice for someone, that kindness sprinkles back on you even bigger and better.

When I heard Dr. Joel Freeman give a presentation on "a white man's journey into black history," I was profoundly struck by his humility, persona, energy, and commitment to helping society achieve equality. As an international theologian, entrepreneur, and author, he is giving, serving, and adding value to individuals and our world at large.

Because my work parallels his, and we speak a similar message of unity and collaboration for the common good of all people, we recognized a profound kinship with each other. That kinship was only strengthened when we learned that we share important interests.

For example, one of my long-term goals is to help build a university-based Center for the Advancement of African American Entrepreneurship in conjunction with an African American Business Hall of Fame and Museum. It will showcase and focus on the past, present, and future contributions of black Americans to the economic development and wealth creation of the United States and ultimately the world. Similarly, Dr. Freeman is working to make public one of the largest and most valued collections of African American artifacts both from historical periods and modern times.

We clicked instantly upon learning that we embrace this common vision. As a result, we concluded that a great museum first needed an outstanding collection of artifacts. Our affirmation of our shared idea added value; together my dream and his dream could create a result greater than the sum of its parts. It's a long-term project, and we are using our combined resources and contacts to bring this vision to life.

The synergy that Joel and I enjoy epitomizes Truth #3—to love, to serve, to give, and to add value to someone or something. We are encouraging each other's dream, and we are giving, serving, and adding value to a unified vision that will benefit thousands of people who visit the museum.

Joel and I cultivate an abundance mentality. We believe that no dream is too big or too bold for us to envision and achieve. And so we take action on a daily basis to create something that will serve and add value to the world. Meanwhile, we are doing that on a smaller scale, every day, with every person we meet. Success in life has everything to do with what we do for others.

Joel shared a story that illustrates how he is living Truth #3 by using his resources and talents to help others. Recently, he and his wife dined at an Italian restaurant with a woman named Lauretta Dorsey Young, whose friendship they had enjoyed for more than three decades. As they savored the meal, Joel reflected on Lauretta's opera singing career, which had taken her around the world and earned her teaching positions at prestigious places such as the Duke Ellington School of Music. But tragedy had silenced Lauretta's beautiful voice when her husband died, leaving her alone to support and raise three daughters. Forced to work at jobs that paid better than her singing gigs, she put her music career on hold.

Success in life has everything to do with what we do for others.

Years later, as Lauretta taught theatre, dance, and music at the Baltimore School for the Arts, Joel suspected that Lauretta's difficult life may have deflated her confidence in herself and in her dream, even now that her daughters were grown and she was free to pursue her passion. This insight motivated Joel to inspire Lauretta to believe in herself once again.

So, over chicken alfredo, Joel spent a half hour outlining a plan for Lauretta to star in a one-woman show. It would feature her portraying through music great African American women such as Harriet Tubman, Phyllis Wheatley, and Sojourner Truth. Joel explained how Lauretta could garner corporate sponsorship to take her unique show around the globe. Then Joel promised Lauretta that he would help guide her to put this plan into action so that she could delight the world with her God-given talent to sing. "I shared thousands of dollars worth of advice," Joel says, "but the excitement dancing in her eyes was priceless."

The "chemistry" that Joel and his wife have shared over the years with Lauretta inspired him to invest his time, energy, and talent to help her. Because of his international contacts, his talents and abilities "fit" with the task of arranging a world tour for an opera singer. And the "timing" of this endeavor was perfect for both Joel and Lauretta. He had the connections and resources to make it happen; she was ready, willing, and available to live her dream. Now, after an elegant garden party to celebrate the debut of her one-woman show, Lauretta is planning to debut her montage of hymns and Negro spirituals in their hometown of Baltimore, Maryland.

Joel says he invested his time and energy to breathe life into her dreams as a karmic gesture of gratitude to the people who have helped him throughout his life. For fifty-three years, other people have been giving, sharing, and adding value to his career and character; he feels it is important to reciprocate that on a grand scale. As a result, he believes that his success is directly proportional to how he helps others. Uplifting people energizes him and instills a sense of peace and purpose that inspires Joel to give, share, and add value to others even more intensely.

Joel recognizes, as well, that he must nurture and tend to all of his relationships—especially the one with his wife: "This morning when my wife was at work, I called her cell phone to let her know that I love her and that I'm thinking of her and I'll be praying for her all day. It took two minutes, but it added value to her day and to our marriage."

Joel compares this to "a love bank." He makes deposits with time, attention, affection, and cards. "If I've made a lot of deposits in the love bank, but I unknowingly make a withdrawal by being inattentive or rushed, then I have a large balance to draw against."

Amazingly, Joel's daily deposits in the "love bank" are earning him much more than cosmic credit toward happiness, fulfillment, and success. He has actually been keeping his body healthier—especially his heart—and prolonging his life!

Love: The Added Benefits

"Fortunately, love protects your heart in ways that we don't completely understand," says highly respected physician Dean Ornish in an article in *Newsweek*. He cites research at top universities that proves this. "In one study at Yale," he says, "men and women who felt the most loved and supported had substantially less blockage in their coronary arteries." According to the article, another study, at Case Western Reserve University, asked 10,000 married men: "Does your wife show her love?" Incredibly, the husbands who answered "yes" had "significantly less angina (chest pain)."

Lack of love is deadly, affirms yet another study, in which researchers at Duke University surveyed people with heart disease. The men and women who were single and lacked close relationships were *three times* more likely to *die* after five years! That is astounding.

"In all three studies, the protective effects of love were independent of other risk factors," concludes the *Newsweek* article. "So if someone says they make you sick, they just might be right." Think about this. Scientific data essentially says that Truth #3 can help you live longer!

Consider my friend Joel. He is adding years to both his life and to the lives of others. Because, while he cultivates a loving environment at home and with friends, he also makes a point to boost the value and self-esteem of strangers. "The small things that you do throughout the day can boost other people's self-confidence," he says. "Sunday evening I purchased a lawnmower at Wal-Mart and a woman named Ramona and a man named Rob provided excellent customer service. I called their manager and praised the way they had helped me. The manager said, 'That's great. Tomorrow morning at our team meeting, I'll showcase them.'"

Joel says he spreads similar encouragement and cheer by logging onto websites for national chain restaurants to laud service he received from certain waiters and waitresses. "It's encouraging to the individual," he says, "especially a younger person. It doesn't take much to . . . help reinforce them in a positive way."

People in general are so desperate for love, service, kindness, and human connection that they will actually pay you for it. Just ask any good waiter, taxi driver, or bartender; they, by far, earn the biggest tips in the service industry. They share the talent of tuning in to what a person is feeling at the moment of contact, be it a couple dining with their young children, a weary traveler just off a long flight, or a hurried business person grabbing a quick lunch. At those moments, the service person's customized assistance can create quick connection and earn him or her greater monetary rewards. This wavelength-sensing ability is a key building block of the Click factor.

> *"The deepest principle in human nature is the craving to be appreciated."*
>
> —psychologist William James

It is something that Joel practices daily, even with telemarketers: "I say, 'I'm not really interested, but I want to encourage you. You've got a tough job but somebody's got to do it. I hope you have a successful day.' " He is living the philosophy of my friend Billie Alice Bowman, who says: "If you're not helping someone, you're just taking up space."

Joel is not only helping Lauretta to launch her career, but he is expanding his efforts to help thousands more people by sharing their story in his book *If Nobody Loves You, Create the Demand* (Authentic Publishing, July 2007). He also shares his wisdom on his website, www.WorkHardWorkSmart.com.

"I get calls all the time from people who want ideas," he says. "I can tell them to read my book first. It's my way of condensing everything to free me up to pursue other things." Joel admits that if he spent all of his time helping others, he would never complete his own work for his consulting business. Declining lunch invitations is a time-saving solution, he says, because it can take half a day to dress for lunch, drive to the restaurant, meet, eat, and drive home. He would rather handle the business in a twenty-minute phone conversation. "It's a matter of setting boundaries," Joel says, "but still being open to reach out to people."

> *"If you're not helping someone, you're just taking up space."*
>
> —Billie Alice Bowman

Have a Positive Impact on Someone's Health, Wealth, or Children

Keith Ferrazzi writes in his wonderful book *Never Eat Alone* of a friendship and mentorship he has with financier-now-philanthropist

Michael Milken. As I was reading the book, I was wowed by this profound and astute quote by Milken: "There are three things in this world that engender deep emotional bonds between people. They are health, wealth, and children." Think about it: those are our most cherished and crucial values. As a result, he says, we experience profound emotions when another person makes a positive impact in these areas of our lives.

Of course, over the last thirty years of teaching, speaking, and writing about networking, I've said the same thing—but not as clearly, succinctly, or categorically as Michael Milken. He is illuminating the core philosophy that master connectors practice daily. That is why asking good questions, listening assertively, and tuning in to people are major Click factors.

> *"There are three things in this world that engender deep emotional bonds between people. They are health, wealth, and children."*
>
> —philanthropist Michael Milken

Here are three things you can do to have a positive impact on someone else's life.

Ask "How Can I Help You Help Me Help You?"

This echoes the famous words of Winston Churchill, who said, "We make a living by what we get, but we make a life by what we give."

However, in our competitive, capitalistic, survival-of-the-fittest world, we are coached to go for the gold as individuals. We think and strategize in terms of "me" and "I." We overlook potentially enriching relationships if they rate low on our "what's in it for me?" scale. But the reality is I need *you* more than you need *me*; I need you so I can give. Only then can I receive. The era of rugged individualism is now giving way to the era of interdependence; this is the highest form of human development.

It's just like what we learned in science class: for every action, there is an equal and opposite reaction. Do something nice for another person and without fail that generosity and kindness will sprinkle back on you at least tenfold.

This concept forces us to think about networking, relationships, and our life goals in a radically new way. We're taught to ask, "What am I going to do to earn my millions?" And when we are awed by people who've already done that by achieving mind-blowing fame and fortune, too often we say, "Wow, look how much money they made!" But we should be saying, "Wow, look at the phenomenal service they are providing to our lives—and how they're being richly rewarded in return."

The ultimate example? Bill Gates. Any article about him includes dollar signs stating his enormous net worth and that of his company, Microsoft.

"We make a living by what we get, but we make a life by what we give."

—Winston Churchill

But do you ever stop to think about the idea that Bill Gates's real legacy is not about money? It's about serving humanity.

He found a way to make computers accessible to the average person. The software that he created served humankind in a way that makes this very complex piece of machinery easy to use in our homes. Bill Gates accomplished that, and by doing so he was serving people—and he was greatly rewarded for his service. Understanding this requires a radical reversal in the way we think. It's a paradigm shift that trains our brains to focus on giving before getting.

The practice of service characterizes a core value in the Mormon community, according to what I have gleaned through articles and conversations. While many religious communities, especially those that have been persecuted, place a huge emphasis on service, the Mormons take this to extraordinary lengths. How? The church assigns members to specific tasks that go far above and beyond common neighborly interaction. The church orchestrates meal deliveries to new mothers, assistance for families that are moving, and social calls. This way, everyone feels connected to and valued by the community.

Imagine if we were all treated to such generous giving and serving in our personal and professional lives! The Mormon community thrives on this spirit of service. And so does—according to my deep belief—our success in life.

Those words ring true for all of us, in business and in life. Everything is about service. Automobile companies build cars to serve people, to get them from point A to point B. As a result, people invest in the type of car they like. When you serve others, whether you are caring for a sick relative, helping a neighbor, or providing a product or professional service through your business, you are cultivating success.

Determine What Value You Bring to the Table

Start by knowing your own worth! You are worthy and deserving of love, appreciation, and financial rewards for your contributions to our world. Valuing ourselves even when the world beats us down with failure, rejection, and criticism brings to mind something I witnessed in an auditorium packed with hundreds of people.

I once observed a young speaker take the stage and wave a $100 bill at the crowd. "Who wants this cash?"

Hands flew up. Shouts echoed off the ceiling.

"Wait." The speaker balled the Benjamin into a wad. Then she held it up between a thumb and forefinger. "Now who wants it?"

The crowd cheered even louder.

"One more thing," she said, tossing the money-ball on the floor. She smashed it under her stiletto heel. Then she pointed at the flat speck on the floor. "Any takers now?"

"Yes! Me!" folks shouted. "I want it!"

The speaker picked up the green and white clump. Unraveled it. Used the edge of the podium to iron it with her palm.

"Look!" she shouted with exuberance. "It's still a hundred bucks! Still worth one hundred dollars. My point here is that life will try to crumple you, smash you to bits, and make you feel worthless. But no matter how bruised or beaten down you feel, your value will never decrease. And people will still want you and love you."

As she so dramatically proved, knowing your value also involves taking inventory of your skills; those talents are the tools with which you can serve. You can start by making a list of the things that you do well. Think about whether you appreciate how those skills boost your confidence and enable you to add value to other people's lives.

Do not think about what's in it for you. Instead, focus on how you can help. The goal is to forget about becoming a person of success; aim to become a person of value. That's when you will start clicking with many more people.

Unfortunately, when I share the concept of "serving," someone always worries that I'm encouraging them to brown-nose. "I'm uncomfortable with this idea of serving," confided a man who approached me after I gave a speech recently on this subject. "Serving," he said, "comes across as kissing people's ass."

"You're exactly right," I said. "It can be perceived in popular culture that way. But if you don't serve, you won't be served. You can get everything in life that you want—if you're willing to help others get what they want first. It's like that old saying, 'What goes around comes around.' " His face lit up with understanding. "Let me warn you," I said. "It's not easy. I've been practicing this for thirty years myself. Practicing, which means I'm not perfect."

To do this, you have to take a risk. You have to ask questions to figure out what people need and want. Only then can you successfully serve . . . and ultimately click.

I serve people when I give a speech. To successfully serve, I must know my audience and what is important to them. Then I can offer information that helps them. In addition, my speeches provide a service to help people understand how to network, connect, and improve their lives. Many people reward my service by buying my books and CDs. But I can't expect you to spend $25 on my books if I don't give you something in return—first.

The only way I'm going to get anything is to connect with people whom I can serve by giving them something that helps them live a better life. Information. Advice. Guidance. A philosophy for success. The more people I serve, the more products or services I can provide, and the more I can be enriched in return.

Let me warn, however, that you must act out of a genuine desire to help others. If you fake it 'til you make it into the big league of success and power, the sophisticated, experienced people you meet will sniff out your insincerity—and evict you from your new seat of power.

"Once you've entered the inner circle of movers and shakers, it behooves you to bring something of value to the table," writes Ed Brown, author of *Build Strategic Relationships with Charisma*. He says most ambitious people make moves up the career ladder that benefit one person: themselves. And they care little about whether their success helps anyone else.

This is wrong, Brown writes. Instead, he advocates behavior that affirms Truth #3 to serve and add value as your primary motive. Every proposal, he says, should emphasize spectacular ways that it benefits the decision-maker. Emphasize how your idea can enhance that person's prosperity and popularity, and you'll create a win-win situation every time.

And unless you approach every endeavor with a spirit of collaboration, Brown writes, " . . . your selfish motives will be uncovered and you will be summarily black-balled from the inner circle as a parasite." A parasite. Think about that. Chances are, you have encountered someone in your personal and professional life who exemplifies this idea of taking, taking, taking to the detriment of the host. Now consider, have you ever felt like a parasite in your relationships? Have you ever put yourself in a situation where your goal was to get something with no regard to what you could give?

Most people probably have. But now, with these truths, you'll be able to change so that you attract peace, productivity, and prosperity. Consider the words of actor Richard Gere as he describes his secrets for success in a *GQ* magazine interview: ". . . if you set your motivation properly, which is to be of service, to make your life an offering, to make it meaningful, then every opportunity to be of service that arises, you're ready to do it." This powerful philosophy requires us to shift our language and our thinking. And that will spark a life-changing transformation to align you with successful people who already get it.

"It behooves you to bring something of value to the table."

—author Ed Brown

Someone who lives this philosophy is Marylin Atkins, chief judge of Detroit's busy 36th District Court. "When I put on my robe, I am a servant of the people who elected me to guarantee justice for our community," she says. "When the governor appointed me, and the people reelected me to this position, they were trusting that I will serve as a voice for them. They trust that I will invest my time, energy, and wisdom to give them fair, courteous service when they come into this building. I am not here to be served like a queen on a throne who collects a nice paycheck every week. I am here every day, all day, to serve the people who elected me, so that their tax dollars are getting them the justice that they deserve."

Judge Atkins is giving without expecting anything in return. She knows that the people who come into her courtroom value justice; she makes herself indispensable to the system by cultivating a reputation for fairness. Outside of work, she makes helping others a priority by taking food to the sick, caring for elderly relatives, and donating clothes and toys to women's shelters. She is winning the game of life by serving and loving others.

The nine mentally and physically disabled children who competed in the 100-yard dash at the Seattle Special Olympics were motivated by the same desire to help. As the children bounded over the starting line they beamed with enthusiasm to run the race and win. But one boy tripped on the asphalt. He tumbled in the wake of the other children and burst into tears.

His sobs caught the attention of the other children. They slowed and turned back to look at him. Then they stopped. And they all swooped back to help the boy. A girl with Down syndrome knelt beside him. "This will make it better," she said, kissing him. With that, the nine children linked arms and proceeded with a triumphant walk to the finish line.

The stadium exploded with cheers as everyone shot to their feet and applauded for a long time. And those who witnessed that tender moment will always share this story as one of the most touching things they have ever seen.

The reason is simple: this story strikes a chord in our hearts about one of the most powerful secrets in life. It is more important to help others win, even if we have to slow down, go backward, and share the victory.

Find Something Positive in Every Person and Situation

I credit my success with this positive and powerful mind-set. What it means is that regardless of the work, I am doing my best. In college, when I was supporting myself by mopping floors at LaGuardia Airport, you better believe they were the cleanest floors in any airport! Whatever I am doing, whomever I am with, I am contributing something positive—adding value.

That—not money—motivates me to do my best. I have never been motivated by money when taking any of the twenty-five jobs I've held over my lifetime. I have always been excited about the task at hand and believed, "Yes, I can add value to this situation."

It is more important to help others win, even if we have to slow down, go backward, and share the victory.

And that includes my very first job, at a grocery store in Brooklyn when I was a teenager.

The manager, Leon, took me down into this dark, dank basement that was crawling with roaches and mice. He told me to sort empty soda bottles, by tossing Coca-Cola, Pepsi, and others into separate containers. The bottles had been returned by customers for the two-cent refund that encouraged recycling. Even though the soda-sorting area was a mess, I was excited.

"I can get this cleaned up," I told Leon. "When can I start?"

"You can start today," he said. Then he paused, staring at me as he started walking up the stairs.

"George," he said, perplexed. "You never asked me how much it paid."

"Oh, how much does it pay?" I asked.

"The minimum wage, $1.25 an hour," he said.

So I got to work. And within two weeks, the place was sparkling.

"Man, this is the best job we've ever had with bottles," Leon said, surveying the basement in amazement. "The way you separated them and made it easy for the soda guys to pick them up is awesome."

I smiled with pride that I had made a valuable contribution to the store and the other workers.

"Would you like to be a stock boy?" Leon asked.

"What does that entail?" I wanted to know.

He took me upstairs, into the bright lights of the supermarket. Pointing to canned peas, corn, and kidney beans, he said, "Stock the shelves so people can find the canned vegetables easily. Starting Monday, you can be the stock boy."

"Great," I said, walking down to the basement.

"George," Leon said, "you never asked how much it paid."

"Okay, how much does it pay?"

"A dollar fifty an hour," Leon said.

The lesson here: In three weeks on the job, my hourly pay jumped from $1.25 to $1.50! And one month later I became the head stock clerk at $2 per hour. All because my goal was to add value. The money naturally follows when we give our services in a spirit of goodwill.

With the next job, I was excited, but I mastered it quickly. Boredom was God's way of telling me that it was time for change. Sometimes life circumstances force us to stay in unfulfilling, challenging situations. I spent nearly thirteen years working for Procter & Gamble so that I could support my family and have a retirement plan and health insurance. I was at first very happy, then bored, then unhappy. I had become different from the people who worked there—not better or worse, just different; I wanted something more. But I was fulfilling my responsibility to my family to provide a comfortable, safe life for them.

Then, when the time was right, I embarked on my entrepreneurial dream to travel the country, writing and speaking about the importance of relationships and networking. I found my purpose. I am adding value to the lives of everyone who hears me speak or reads my books. And in return, my life is enriched with spiritual, emotional, and financial rewards.

The truth is, if you can leave your job today and be happy about it, you are in the wrong job. You are not living your life on purpose and you are wasting precious time. Often I say to people, "Do anything, but don't waste my time. I will get more money, but I will not get any more time. I don't know how much time I have, and I don't want to know, but don't you waste it." That way, I can invest my time in adding value to yours.

What gift(s) are you holding hostage from your community because of your personal fears?

Exercise for Truth #3

Mentoring is one of the most powerful ways that you can enhance another person's life. Think about how your mentors have guided and nurtured you over the years and how grateful you feel that they helped elevate your personal and professional endeavors. Now, figure out how you can cast similarly powerful karma back on others by being an outstanding mentor.

Here are some specific ways that you can do that:

1. Make a list of helpful people that you can connect with your mentees to advance their careers.

Mentee	Helpful Person	Benefit
1.		
2.		
3.		
4.		
5.		

2. Boost your mentees' self-confidence by providing positive feedback for their strengths.

Mentee	Positive Skills, Habits, Goals
1.	
2.	
3.	
4.	
5.	

3. Help your mentees improve by offering constructive criticism. For example, if you notice that your mentee has a bad habit of procrastinating, offer tips for better time management. And if you see that your mentee lacks confidence, find ways to cultivate his self-esteem.

Mentee	Criticism	Ways to Improve
1.		
2.		
3.		
4.		
5.		

Key **CLICK** Factors

Add Value
♦ Make having an impact on someone's wealth, health, or children a priority.
♦ Know what the people you deal with value.

◆ Make yourself aware of their needs.

◆ Give with no strings attached.

◆ Have an abundance mentality.

◆ Make yourself indispensable.

Always

◆ Be the first to help and do it with kindness.

◆ Push your pride and ego aside.

◆ Be willing to receive when the offer to help is extended to you.

Keep in Mind

◆ You can get everything in life you want, if you're willing to help others get what they want first.

◆ Everything that is good may not be right for you at that time.

Do Not

◆ Think only about what's in it for you. Rather, think about how you can add value to someone or something.

◆ Instead of trying to become a person of success become a person of value.

Make Sure To

◆ Follow through once you begin to help.

◆ Never lose the lessons life teaches us, because in life we either win or learn, but we never lose. If we miss the lesson, we are bound to repeat it until we learn it.

Nurture Your Relationships— and Yourself

Send someone a signal that they matter.

—Isaiah 50:4a

THE IMPORTANT RELATIONSHIPS in your life—whether with a spouse, business partner, or friend—require commitment. With this in mind, you should take every opportunity to cultivate happiness and trust in these relationships. Even when you first meet people, strive to make them feel special, to feel that you're genuinely interested in them and their life.

How? Get personal. Ask about their children, their work, their love life, their hobbies. Let your curiosity and compassion guide conversations that let them trust you. People will forget what you say and do, but they will not forget how you make them feel loved and appreciated. Truth #4 is about tending to, sustaining, and pampering your relationships—all with the intention to "click" up to higher and higher levels of trust, friendship, prosperity, and joy.

Imagine you are a musician who has been hustling to score your "big break"—and the seven-figure check that comes with it. For years, your talent and tenacity have turbocharged your dream of escaping the nightmarish poverty of your young life. You persist, even as you navigate a treacherous terrain of people whose unscrupulous and dishonest promises have rewarded you with no record deals and zero dollars.

Now fathom the idea of a powerful music industry executive offering you a three million dollar recording contract. But your lawyer tells you to reject the offer.

That lawyer would be Darrell Miller, a Beverly Hills entertainment attorney whose unique brand and background enable him to make powerful connections with many Hollywood heavyweights and stars. With amazing finesse, he thrives in a category of business relationships that can be sometimes prickly, sensitive, and narcissistic.

Darrell possesses a combination of professional rigor and collegiality. His body language matches his words because both are genuine. He is comfortable and confident, some would say charismatic. Darrell is naturally kind, empathetic, and curious, with a strong work ethic and an easy smile. At the same time, he's the kind of guy who can let his guard down just a bit to allow others in. And his ego won't get in the way of learning.

Because Darrell is a master at pampering relationships, those connections evolve into loyal, long-term alliances with superstar performers as well as producers and executives at studios and production companies. What also enables Darrell to click with this entertainment elite is that he understands the art of the deal from both sides of the negotiating table.

Darrell Miller was once a classically trained opera singer. And his mother, Angel Miller, was a gospel vocalist who influenced his education at a performing arts high school and Cincinnati's College Conservatory of Music.

While enchanting audiences around the globe with his voice, the young Darrell experienced an epiphany in India. He realized that with a law degree, he could bolster his creative experiences with legal expertise—and become an entertainment attorney extraordinaire.

Nearly two decades later, his epiphany has proven prophetic, because Darrell connects so profoundly with his clients that he can, in fact, convince the ambitious, young musician to turn down the multimillion-dollar contract for a short-term smaller deal. "The three million dollar record deal may give them their first fifteen minutes of fame," says Darrell, playing on the phrase coined by the late artist Andy Warhol, "but it is my responsibility to prepare my clients for their sixteenth minute of fame."

That philosophy is the essence of how Darrell pampers his relationships. His personal experiences, plus his professional expertise, enable him to spare talented people from the "starving artist" tragedy. Instead, the forty-three-year-old managing partner at Miller & Pliakas law firm grooms his clients to achieve their maximum potential, both financially and creatively.

"To tell someone, 'You're better off not taking the three million,' and have them still trust you," Darrell says, "that is difficult. But my practice is about thinking beyond the box so that I can help my clients achieve long-term success by building and maintaining brands."

Darrell explains that for some people it is more beneficial to secure a record deal that will ensure artistic and financial longevity by receiving smaller payments spread over several years, rather than a lump-sum payment of three million dollars. "The client will say, 'But I need the money now!' Or they'll ask, 'What are you talking about! Is there a guarantee I'll still get paid? How do you know?!' "

Darrell *knows* they will get paid. He helped craft a twenty-five million dollar, three-picture deal at Warner Brothers for the rapper DMX, which set a precedent for urban music artists at a time in Hollywood when they were not so welcome to become movie stars. With many award-winning, famous, and connected loyal clients, Darrell is working as legal counsel to the rich and famous.

Darrell says it can be challenging to watch young artists who are often the first generation of wealth in their families, because they arrive at the negotiating table in Hollywood without a clue as to how to develop and sustain a career in the entertainment and sports business.

"The idea of believing you'll get more than the three million in front of you is often the most challenging decision many people will make in their lifetime," Darrell says. Another problem? The super-glamorous "bling!" of pop culture's music videos, song lyrics, and youth-targeted films condemns the nouveau riche to a "I-want-to-get-paid" cash-consumer mentality. "There have been reports of a person getting a five million dollar check and immediately buying five Rolls Royces," Darrell says, "or diamond-studded platinum Rolex watches for everyone in his posse. We've seen people buy multiple homes and the best of everything, without knowing what property taxes are."

Sadly, Darrell has watched too many talented artists skyrocket from poverty to fame and fortune, only to crash backward into bankruptcy just as quickly. So how does he convince the musician to turn down the big bucks and accept a deal for smaller payments spread over several years? With common sense and by staying focused on one's plan for success.

Darrell warns them about becoming a rags-to-riches-to-rags story. With that said, the entertainers calm down and listen to his advice. He encourages them to opt for the longer-term deals as a strategy for building and generating real wealth. And it works. He says the proof is in the profits. "I've taken many artists from having one revenue stream to having seven or eight streams of income."

But what is it about Darrell's style that permits him to garner so much loyalty and trust that clients seek counsel and advice on the most sensitive business matters? Darrell says he educates his clients about financial planning and strategic thinking for long-term success.

Darrell knows that having an impact on someone's wealth in a long-term, positive way creates chemistry and deep bonding—a click. So how does Darrell Miller maintain respect in the sometimes wicked world of entertainment where everyone loves the A-list celebrities but few adore the scandal-plagued, rebellious falling stars?

Darrell credits the hands-on personal attention that he lavishes on each client—especially when trouble strikes. "You would be surprised that sometimes superstar clients in the middle of multi-million dollar movie productions engage in conduct that results in a picture being shut down for a day or more," Darrell says. "This could cost a studio two or three million dollars per day, depending on the project. When artists clash with studios or networks, there are often threats of lawsuits over who would be responsible for the cost and many threats about the fate of the artist's career." During those times, he says, he shifts from his typical role and becomes a therapist, social worker, and big brother for his movie star client.

"I remember one time when I had to work it all out and stay calm in an effort that a client would not be destroyed by the studio, which would have made my client the scapegoat," Darrell says. "I defused that situation by going into the trailer and calmly speaking to my client to explain the big picture. I enabled my client to see how this behavior would impact one's career, and we were able to resolve the conflict."

Darrell says another time a client's viewpoint was criticized as so politically incorrect that a major corporation had threatened to cancel the performer's multimillion-dollar endorsement deal. Darrell says he succeeded in convincing the corporation to honor the endorsement contract.

Two important values inspire Darrell's techniques for pampering relationships with clients and friends. "No matter how excited we are to work together, the two words that I flatly tell people are: loyalty and respect. I have to earn your loyalty and respect. Respect is not something you get on the first day. It's something that you earn over time. The fact that my firm recently celebrated ten years in business, with many long-term clients, shows that we are earning that loyalty and respect by the way that we nurture our relationships."

Our number one responsibility to one another is to nurture and build each other's self-esteem and self-confidence.

Darrell Miller is successful in business and in life because he understands that our number one responsibility to one another is to nurture and build each other's self-esteem and self-confidence. We do this by connecting on an emotional and spiritual level—and by giving love.

And that simple act adds value to people's lives. While he helps artists build wealth through their careers, he is also helping men and women appreciate their value as human beings. Because self-worth goes hand-in-hand with self-esteem.

When we believe we are worthy of wealth and love and success, then the spiritual laws of the universe respond accordingly by showering us with riches and rewarding personal relationships. And to attract great relationships that we can develop into a lifetime of business, we must first nurture ourselves to think outside the box.

Pamper Yourself First

Who is the most important person in your life? You!

I don't say this to suggest that you should be self-centered or egotistical. But you can only be the best mother, lawyer, father, CEO, brother, team captain, or artist if you take excellent care of yourself. Being a living picture of health is appealing to most people, and that sets you up for a peak and inspired performance.

"Our body is a machine for living," wrote the great writer and philosopher Leo Tolstoy. But if we neglect or abuse our machines, they break down. If they don't conk out entirely, our bodies force us to fix them. Repairs and recuperation slow us down. They sideline us at pit stops where we must assess and repair the damage, and craft a better maintenance plan. As a result, breakdowns usually inspire us to take better care of these magnificent machines so that we may continue our race for success.

Public relations superstar Terrie Williams is living proof that failure to pamper oneself can take a terrible toll on one's mind, body, and spirit.

Yes, her morning-to-midnight schedule and her awesome work ethic and her indomitable drive made her New York public relations firm sparkle with the most coveted celebrity clients. Yes, she was earning a spectacular salary. And yes, she built a stellar reputation among stars like Eddie Murphy as *the* person to call to promote events.

"The price I paid was depression," says the fifty-four-year-old author of *The Personal Touch*, which is the ultimate guide to pampering relationships in business and in life. "I spent years and years of giving and doing for everybody else, but not me. I was the last thing considered."

Terrie Williams was neglecting her magnificent machine. In her robotic quest for success, she had disconnected from her mind, body, and spirit. "You think you're doing okay, but you're not. At some point, the mask is going to crack. That is the great cost for constantly putting everybody else before you."

Terrie wasn't even allowing herself time for basic necessities. "You know when you have to go to the bathroom and it's ten-thirty in the morning, but you have one more meeting, one more phone call, one more this, and one more that?" Terrie asks. "And then you look up and it's four in the afternoon and you still have to go to the bathroom?"

Terrie says she ignored her body's needs because she was so focused on devoting every minute to work. She was obsessed with dominating her competition and living up to her superstar reputation by pleasing her high-profile clients. But her bad habits contributed to depression. And the mental illness forced her to reconnect with her brain, her body, and her spiritual self.

To change her behavior, Terrie has had to re-script her inner dialogue. If she finds herself slipping back into bad habits, she acknowledges the issues: " 'Are you really going to lose that much time by stopping and going to the restroom? Or if you postpone or cancel this meeting, is it really such a horrible thing?' I ask myself the question and I take the time to listen."

The answer? "There's a part of me that says, 'Oh no, you made this commitment. You have to honor that.' But if somebody ends up not doing business with me because I decided I needed to honor myself, then it doesn't matter."

Terrie's new mind-set also requires changing the way she thinks about time. She celebrates the small victories, such as resisting the temptation to add one more appointment to an already stacked daily schedule. "We do that because we think we'll miss something," she says. "There's competition to be the best, the superman, the superwoman. But there's no such thing. You're not going to get off scot-free by stretching yourself too thin."

Terrie says she uses her frequent public speaking engagements to share these messages, which resonate with many listeners. "At first people think I'm crazy," Terrie says, "but then they say, 'You know what? Every time I go to the bathroom, I think about you.' I tell them that is a victory because you are honoring yourself at the most basic level."

Along with personal anecdotes, Terrie also says she constantly reminds people of the warning that flight attendants give.

"It bears reminding oneself of ten times a day that when you are in a plane and there's a need for oxygen, the mask drops down and you are to put it over your own mouth first," Terrie says. "Then if you have a small child next to you or somebody acting like a small child, then and only then are you even able to secure their mask. After you have secured yours."

> *"You cannot do anything for anybody else unless you are taking care of yourself first."*
>
> —public relations professional
> Terrie Williams

Terrie had heard flight attendants say those words countless times. But one day, after depression struck, the message resonated with profound power. "It's so symbolic for life," she says. "You cannot do anything for anybody else unless you are taking care of yourself first."

Terrie, however, was not doing that, especially when it came to our most fundamental need: eating. "Food was my addiction," she says. "I would eat whatever, with no structure to it." She says junk food and giant portions sent her weight soaring.

But when depression forced her to examine her lifestyle, she vowed to nurture her body with healthy food. Now, every morning, a cuisine service delivers three healthy meals and two snacks to her home in New York City. She says the fruits, vegetables, whole grains, and low-fat fish and meats are rejuvenating her body. And she feels more energetic and slim.

Before her diagnosis for depression, for which she takes medication, Terrie says exercise failed to rank anywhere on her daily agenda. Now she works out with a personal trainer three times every week. "I thought I could eat healthy and exercise by myself, but I realized I wasn't doing it. Something would always come in front of me, always. Even now, I sometimes arrive at the gym five or ten minutes late—and it's downstairs in my building!" Terrie says paying a trainer motivates her to attend each session because she gets billed whether she shows up or not. "I'm going to be there for me to stay healthy and whole."

Terrie's self-pampering regimen does not end after meals and workouts. "I can do nothing without God in my life," she says. "Nurturing my spirit is key. I don't feel whole or connected if I don't go to church on Sundays to get that spiritual message."

A recent experience proved just how hungry her spirit was, when her extensive travel schedule kept her away from her favorite church for two months. "I felt an emptiness, a real void," she says. "Feeding the spirit is as important as feeding yourself physically every day." In fact, Terrie believes that her depression may be rooted in her lack of an outlet for her emotionally draining work.

Now, church is that outlet. For example, she recently did a pro bono speech for The Innocence Project, which freed 180 innocent people from prison with DNA evidence. "One guy went in at sixteen and came out twenty-four years later for something he didn't do," Terrie recalls. "I can't tell you what it did to be in a room to hear those stories. It was more than I could take." After that, Terrie flew back to New York and attended her favorite church, where she walked in as a hymn was being sung. She remembered the wrongly convicted prisoners' heartbreaking stories.

"The tears were streaming down my cheeks and I said, 'This is where I need to be.' " Releasing intense emotions, Terrie says, is key to pampering herself, so that they do not fester and cause illness such as depression.

Too often, she says, "Successful people move like lightning and don't process the things that happen. We're on to the next thing. You suffer for a moment and don't get it out. But that stuff festers. You self-medicate through work, food, shopping, drugs, or alcohol. You have to go somewhere with it, whether it's a therapist or church."

Now that Terrie is eating healthfully, exercising, and nourishing her spirit, she indulges one more way to pamper herself. "I'm a person who needs quiet time," she says. "If I don't get that, I'm not right with the world." Terrie cherishes solitude on Sundays, when she retreats to the silence and stillness of her home to read, write in her journal, watch TV, and replenish her energy.

All the while, Terrie indulges her passion only on projects that are fulfilling and purposeful. Right now, she and a business partner are running a recording studio on ten acres in New York where artists live and work on creative projects. She's also writing another book. And she's mentoring a former gang member who now lives legally and peacefully by helping young people.

Terrie says pampering herself and encouraging others to do the same enables her to feel much better as she pursues her life passions. "These are things I was called to do," she says, "And I can't do those things if I'm not healthy." Terrie knows better than most of us that we must pamper ourselves before we can pamper our relationships with others.

Strengthen Your Brand

What is the number one brand for You, Inc.?

Let me clarify about branding: Coca-Cola is one of the world's favorite soft drinks, Crest is a popular toothpaste, and Godiva is exquisite chocolate.

But the top brand at You, Inc. isn't a product. Just as your voice is not the literal sound that comes out of your mouth, your brand is not necessarily a literal symbol. Your brand is your reputation. What you are known for.

So what can you do to make your " brand" something that will make people happy? Something so powerful and unforgettable that when you call or they hear your name, they automatically smile? What can you do to create a reputation that will make them enjoy doing business with you and look forward to the next time you seal a deal together?

You can cultivate a reputation for spreading happiness, good cheer, and an optimistic attitude. Remember, reputation is what people know and think about you, even if they've never met you. It's the verbal character sketch that gets passed from lips to ears in elevators, bars, fitness clubs, restaurants, and boardrooms.

Your reputation is the feeling that you arouse in people, whether good or bad. It is what you are known for—delivering flawless projects on time; baking the sweetest, melt-in-your-mouth birthday cakes for friends and family; or always having an uplifting, eloquent pep talk for anyone who's down.

I have one friend who, despite horrific personal tragedy, has a smile like a sunburst, with a sunny outlook to match, and quick words of wisdom that brighten even the quickest exchanges. He could be a janitor or a judge. But his personal brand is infectious happiness that delights everyone he encounters. His secret? Regardless of his trade or circumstances in life, selling himself as a human being, connecting to other people with the most primal universal greeting of a smile, shows love and adds value to people's lives. That is his brand: infectious cheer, empathy, and compassion.

Some people—cynics—might call it ingratiating or brown-nosing or sucking up. But the bottom line is that saying and doing things that make other people feel good reflects back on you with infinite brilliance. So you should always:

♦ **Be nice to strangers.** What if that anonymous person at the mall—the one you stole the parking spot from—turns out to be your boss someday? What if the couple who complained about your drunken, boisterous behavior at the restaurant Saturday night is your star client and her husband? What if that store clerk you yelled at for mixing up your order turns out to be your cousin's fiancé?

As far as your behavior goes, you are always punched in on the success clock. That's why you should treat all people, everywhere, every day, with kindness and compassion. They say all humans are linked by only six degrees of separation; in many circles, the degrees are much smaller. The bottom line: it's a small world, and everybody is connected somehow. And you only want them to know good things about you. So keep your sterling reputation sparkling by polishing it with words and acts of kindness for everyone you meet. In other words, pamper strangers, too!

+ **Lavish praise and gratitude.** To the man mopping the lobby floor: "Wow, it's really sparkling in here!" To the waitress who got your special order correct: "I appreciate your tender loving care for my order. It's delicious." Send a thank-you note to the overworked ER nurse who took care of your sprained ankle. I remember a friend sent a beautiful card to the hospital staff who had treated her double pneumonia. The nurses were shocked and thrilled; few people, they said, ever took time to say thank you for making them healthy again. A simple compliment or expression of gratitude can brighten anyone's outlook. Yours might be the first kind words that person has heard all day. And you may be watering their seeds of hope that were scorched by criticism or cruelty.

+ **Make 'em laugh!** This is one of the best ways to connect with an individual or an audience. Tell a quick joke. Laughing releases endorphins that make us happier and healthier. New acquaintances often say, after we've shared a laugh, "George, I feel like I've known you for ten years." And that sense of depth makes them want to cultivate a connection that grows into friendship and/or business collaboration.

  I'm great at topical humor and ad-libbing. I like to find the spontaneous humor in everyday situations. At times when people ask me to do something, I'll say, "Do you want fries with that?" Or when I'm writing a check at a grocery store, I'll write on the memo line, "For Smuggling Diamonds," or finish a nondescript sentence with "in Accordance With the Prophecy." Other times, I specify that my drive-through order is "To Go." I once told my two sons at the dinner table, "Due to the economy, we are going to have to let one of you go." Yes, anything for a good laugh! It just makes me and the other party feel good.

♦ **Keep in touch!** Technology makes it easy to stay connected with friends, family, and professional contacts. Cell phones and e-mail give us anytime access; weekly lunches or coffee chats keep us communicating while sharing ideas and encouragement. Sure we can "park" some relationships; we don't need to talk to everyone in our network more than a few times a year. But don't just call people when you need something; that's a big turn-off. Find ways to let them know you're thinking of them: clip that magazine article about his favorite vacation spot and drop it in the mail; e-mail her an uplifting note; pass along a coupon you received for your friend's favorite Indian restaurant.

Octavius "Ted" Reid III, senior vice president at Morgan Stanley, sends out thousands of free four-page newsletters six times a year to his clients and friends in the sports and entertainment industry. The newsletters are packed with valuable investment information that many investment newsletters charge for. I call this "dripping goodwill."

This is an important practice at our company as well; our *PowerNetworking Minute* reaches sixty thousand people each week by e-mail. The useful tips, facts, and ideas about networking are a way to serve and add value to the lives of our customers. Effective networkers like Ted understand that's the way to make the connections and then over time . . . Click!

Stay in the Moment

Some of the most charismatic people of our time—such as former President Bill Clinton—have a magic touch with people. Why?

Because people like President Clinton make you feel like you're the only person in the room for that moment. His eyes focus directly into your eyes. He's listening to what you say. He's feeling your pain or your compassion. And you walk away from that exchange—even if it lasted only a few minutes—feeling as if you deeply connected with him. Mr. Clinton developed his natural charisma into an unforgettable magnetism that was so powerful it helped him win two terms as president of the United States.

You can have this impact on people, too, by focusing solely on them. Do not look around the room to see who else is there. Do not look at your cell phone or your watch. Do not close your eyes (some people have this habit and it makes me feel "shut out"—like they don't want to visually connect with me). Look into their eyes. Shake their hand and hold it. Feel their energy.

Darrell Miller says staying in the moment with his clients helps them feel comfortable and confident that they will prevail over a crisis: "I stay in the moment. When I'm talking to you, I'm talking to you." But he says our high-tech, multitasking lifestyles interfere. "Something is always ringing or buzzing or competing to take our attention away from the people we're with."

To combat interruptions, Darrell says he lavishes each client with his undivided attention by shutting the office door, instructing assistants to indulge him and his client with privacy, and turning off his cell phone so that it does not ring during the conversation. "That shows my clients that I am there in the moment with them."

And that individual attention, he says, is the most important way to pamper relationships and create more "click" moments.

Exercise for Truth #4

If you're not taking care of yourself, you can't take care of others. That means you can't click or build extraordinary relationships if you're neglecting the number one person in your life—you! So promise to nurture yourself every day—in mind, body, and spirit—so that you can offer your best self to the world.

Take an honest inventory of your lifestyle:

1. **Mind.** Is your brain a cyclone of cynicism? Does it churn with worry and pessimism all day long? Does it reel with anxiety, even when you close your eyes to sleep? List three ways that you can calm your mind. They can include soothing music, exercise, prayer, laughter, and so on. Promise that you will utilize these tools throughout the day to calm your mind. Only then can you achieve your maximum potential to click with other people and enjoy great relationships.

2. **Body.** You hear it constantly, because it's the gospel. Without health, you have nothing. Poor health habits will make you sluggish, cranky, unattractive, and downright sick. And none of those will help you succeed. So promise yourself that you will take excellent care of the amazing machine that enables you to enjoy life: your body! Do you eat at least five servings of fruits and vegetables a day? Are you overweight? Are you making an effort to lose weight to achieve maximum energy and exuberance? Do you get at least seven hours of sleep every night? Do you exercise? Do you groom yourself for a pleasant appearance? Are you clean and smelling fresh?

3. **Heart.** Our hearts are an internal radar system that guides us to say and do the right things. We should use this intuitive power to make decisions, cultivate relationships, and work toward goals. So turn inward and ask: Do I listen to my heart? Do I consider the strong influences of my heart when meeting people, making decisions, and setting goals? Have I shut off my heartfelt feelings? Am I afraid of the truths that my heart speaks? How

can I open myself up to listen to what my heart is telling me and act accordingly? What can I do throughout the day to remind myself to quiet the noise and listen to the answers that are literally beating inside me?

4. **Spirit.** Strong spiritual beliefs are the key to the most prosperous, productive, and peaceful life. Take a moment to ask yourself: How strong are your spiritual beliefs? How do you connect with God or a higher power? Do you meditate? Pray? What can you do throughout the day to connect most intimately with God or your higher power?

Key **CLICK** Factors

Always
- See the strengths, not the limitations, in others.
- Befriend people for who they are, not for what they can do for you.
- Put aside your ego, and make someone better with you than they would be with anyone else.

Keep in Mind
- Under everyone's hard shell is someone who wants to be appreciated and loved. Make them feel good through a sincere display of interest, empathy, and compassion, where appropriate.

Do Not
- Ask people to do something in conflict with their values or something they are not capable of doing.

Make Sure To

◆ Always display a sense of humor. Everyone you meet deserves to be greeted with a smile; plus, it's an inexpensive way to improve your looks!

PART 2

FIT

Fit *adjective, verb, noun*
1. To be adapted to or suitable for a purpose, object, or occasion
2. Worthy or deserving
3. Prepared or ready
4. Qualified or competent as for an office or function
5. Proper and becoming
6. To adjust or make conform to something
7. To put with precise placement or adjustment

Adapted from *Dictionary.com Unabridged (v 1.1)*.
Random House, Inc.

You may enjoy an immediate and overwhelming explosion of chemistry with another person, but you must also experience a good "fit" for the relationship to flourish. For example, if a man and a woman click and sparks fly, when they're both single and searching for a soul mate, then they have a perfect fit.

What exactly is a "perfect fit"? Chances are, you've mentioned a good friend, associate, or lover and said: "I can't put my finger on why we get along so well. We're just a perfect fit." But if you can't put it into words, how can you make sure that your perfect fit survives and thrives?

The answer: by applying Truth #5: Bless Them and Release Them, Truth #6: Trust First; Distrust Must Be Earned, and Truth #7: Tailor Your Relationships for the Perfect Fit to all of your relationships. These Truths articulate how you can cultivate a precise fit so that you can create and celebrate extraordinary relationships in business and in life.

First, Truth #5 warns that we must rigorously regulate our relationships. That means, if and when the passion dies, the partnership crumbles, or the friendship deteriorates, we must courageously say good-bye to that person. We must prune our proverbial relationship trees of toxic branches so that positive new connections can blossom in our lives. In the process, we must be grateful for the life experience—the love, the romance, the business deal, the lessons learned—that this person provided. When we bless and release past relationships—and refuse to allow bitterness to poison our memories of them—we create space to click with even better chemistry among new friends, loved ones, and business associates.

Doing that successfully enables us to enter new relationships in a spirit of trust and optimism. So, rather than carry the cynical baggage of past relationships-gone-bad into new connections, Truth #6 recommends that we trust first, and only distrust if someone says or does something to rouse our suspicions.

Achieving this is an inside job; it is only possible by trusting ourselves first—that we are on purpose, that we are adding value, and that the universe will help us click with upbeat, positive people who shine happiness, fulfillment, and prosperity into our lives.

Then, once we click with a new person, the best way to endear ourselves in their hearts, business plans, and social calendars is to utilize Truth #7. It recommends that we tailor our relationships for the perfect fit. By doing so, we are honoring their unique preferences, styles, and tastes. We are also cultivating the perfect fit that simply feels right—for business or for pleasure. It should feel natural, never forced, and sincere, never phony.

And so, when we release the old, trust the new, and tailor our words and actions to each individual, we click to create the perfect fit for extraordinary relationships.

Ways to Enhance Fit
- Be open
- Listen
- Be flexible
- Be adaptable
- Be curious
- Be experimental
- Find out what's important to the person
- Serve
- Be knowledgeable

Bless Them and Release Them

A relationship is like a shark. It has to constantly move forward or it dies.

—Woody Allen's character in *Annie Hall*

SUCCESS REQUIRES TEAMING up with people who share our values and principles, not people who are toxic or self-serving. So if you want to change your life, change your relationships! Your five best friends tell the world who you are based on their values, principles, and lifestyles. This team fits you and will either lift you up or pull you down. If life is a tree, and your friends and associates are branches, prune the toxic ones so the rest can get stronger and grow the sweetest fruit. Don't spend major time with minor people.

Nina Brown had the kind of lover who was as sexy and enchanting as the men she writes about in her romantic novels. Newly divorced after a decade of monogamy, the thirty-something author says she was savoring every sensuous second of erotic indulgence with her new man.

This young, athletic Adonis named Damion was the most succulent fruit on her relationship tree. But even that couldn't save him from the pruning shears. "He seemed like a golden apple on the surface," Nina says years later. "But it was fake, a façade, an intoxicating illusion. And after a few bites, I realized I was tasting bitter flavors in him that were actually sour spots within myself. But I ultimately wanted to get real, then move onward and upward."

Over the past three years, I've watched Nina do just that. When we met, she had just begun to prune the toxic branches from her relationship tree and replace them with inspiring, vibrant new ones. When I was invited to speak at a charitable event, Nina and I immediately connected on the level of common values, visions, and goals. I was speaking a language that she needed to hear.

Over the years, I've watched her put my principles to work to dramatically improve her life on every level. So I invited her to share how she found the strength to prune the most luscious fruit from her relationship tree to create a more peaceful, prosperous, and purposeful life.

"Damion and I clicked instantly," says Nina, who chose not to use either her real name nor her former lover's real name for this story, owing to the personal nature of her testimony. "At the moment, the chemistry, fit, and timing seemed perfect. But looking back, our relationship showed how you can think you're connecting on a deep level, but once you take a closer look and see the real person beneath the façade, you can disconnect just as quickly."

Nina admits, "Damion was like an addiction. Intoxicating at first, but in the end, not good for me." When she met him at a black-tie party, he was impeccably dressed in a tuxedo, with a fresh manicure and flawless grooming. The consummate gentleman, he impressed her with his humorous philosophy on life and love.

"We connected," Nina recalls, "because it seemed like we had similar ambitions and perspectives." Then he bedazzled her with fantasy dates, the kind you see in the movies: Talking about Shakespeare while lifting weights at the gym. Dancing the night away. Watching romantic movies. Having picnics in the park.

"He was like opium for the senses—gorgeous, deep voice with articulate words, sensuous touch, delicious taste, amazing cologne," Nina says. "We had the kind of electricity that, when I closed my eyes, I literally saw silver stars."

A former newspaper reporter, Nina says Damion seemed impressed by her vision of a future glittering with fame and fortune as a writer. He praised her accomplishments—writing books, earning degrees from major universities, and appearing on national television shows.

But, she adds, something in her gut was warning her: all that glitters is not gold. Like when he'd suddenly cancel their plans at the last minute. Sometimes he just wouldn't show up or even call for days. Other times, his "business meeting" would drag into the wee hours. Or he'd say he had an engagement to attend at midnight—without her.

"There was a disconnect between the fantasy that Damion cast around himself and the reality of what I was starting to see," Nina says. "And every incident was like a little ax chipping away at the connection I thought we had."

Another problem? Damion would look in the mirror and say, "I'm such a loser. What are you doing with me?" Although he had outward symbols of success—a nice house and car, beautiful clothes, and lots of cash—sometimes his cell phone would get cut off for a week at a time, as if he hadn't paid his bill.

And once, when she arrived to find his home looking like the aftermath of a lovers' tryst—*two* used champagne glasses, an empty bottle, Chinese take-out cartons, and two wet towels in his bathroom—he claimed that he'd indulged in all that by himself. "I don't deserve you," he'd say playfully. "I can't believe you really want me."

Also, the opulent business projects that Damion boasted about would never come to fruition. He'd claim that an investor pulled out of the deal. Or he was still waiting on financing for another endeavor. A paperwork glitch put negotiations on hold. And his plans to go back to school for his master's degree kept getting delayed by missed deadlines or a scheduling change with his business.

Suddenly furious, he'd say he trusted no one, that everyone had a sinister motive for wanting to befriend you or partner with you, and that it was only a matter of time before seemingly cool people yanked off their masks to reveal monsters within.

"All these giant red flags about the real Damion were waving right in my face," Nina confesses. "But romance has a way of blinding you to reality." Until one evening when he greeted her at his door with a fireplace blazing behind him. The seductive scene swept her away from disappointment over a failed book deal and financial worries.

"My state of mind, post-divorce, had me craving some type of escape, too," she says. "I was two thoughts away from panic. My career was stalled, I was depressed, and I didn't really know what I wanted. I didn't know who I was outside of an author and a newly single woman."

Her mind was a dizzying jumble of question marks. And her quest for answers inspired praying, journaling, and reading books such as *Real Magic* by Dr. Wayne Dyer, who asserts that our relationships reflect who we are. Then, she says, she realized that in

order to change her life, she needed to begin by changing her relationships, starting with Damion.

So, in the midst of Damion's kiss, she pulled back and studied
his gorgeous face. She asked herself, If eyes are the windows to our
souls, and our relationships mirror who we are, then what are we
supposed to see when we gaze into our lover's eyes?

"You're not supposed to cringe, like I did," Nina says. "Something
flickered back at me from his eyes that I once found so enchanting,
and this awful feeling in my gut twisted like a knife."

She realized that her illusory connection with Damion was an
intoxicating distraction from facing all the stuff she needed to
unravel in her own life. It was much more fun to get lost in the
euphoria of Damion's passionate phone messages, the anticipation
of their next tryst, the detailed remembrances of recent ones, and
the worry about who Damion really was—and what he was doing
when he wasn't with Nina. Thinking about him was easier than
trying to figure out who she really was.

Since deception had plagued her marriage, Nina had stopped
believing in honesty in relationships. "I had the extremely cynical
attitude that everybody is hiding something, and when it comes to
sex, everybody lies to pretend they're endorsing what I called 'the
myth of monogamy.' "

She also believed that any man like Damion—young, professional, single—would have women throwing themselves at him
all day long. So why bother faking the lie of exclusivity? "I knew
my mind-set was out of whack when I defined trust as 'trusting
that Damion practices safe sex with the other women he's sleeping
with.' "

Plus, married men, Nina says, were always asking her for dates.
Or lavishing her with romantic dinners, *then* revealing that they
had a wife! Business associates, too, would propose elaborate
collaborations that never materialized, despite her follow-up. "I

thought I was connecting with people, but they weren't giving me any encouragement to trust the face value of words," she says, "because their actions did the lying for them."

Nina says, in this day of HIV, when "you're literally putting your life in someone's hands when you go to bed with them," both she and Damion agreed to get tested for HIV and other STDs. Both negative, they practiced safe sex together. "But sex was really all I wanted from him. So was I using him? Was he using me? Was that okay?"

No, she decided as she stared into his eyes. They mirrored the distrust and dishonesty that she knew was radiating from her own eyes. "I was lying to myself. People kept asking, 'How's your novel coming?' And I'd fib that I was working away on it. The truth was, I was so shell-shocked from the divorce and recent career disappointments, and the financial mess that it all created, that my writing was paralyzed."

At that moment, she also saw in Damion's eyes that his seeming lack of commitment to himself, to her, and to his career reflected how she wasn't committed to herself either. Not to figuring out why her marriage failed, how to get her career back on track, or how to manifest success for her mind, body, and spirit.

Her heart ached for love. And though, at first, it seemed they had connected in the most intimate way, even the thrill of passion left her feeling empty with heartache. "I think we connected because we were both disconnected inside," Nina says.

As she turned inward to find answers, she realized that the sexy, adventurous spirit that she thought was authentic in Damion was just as much a mask as the bubbly exuberance she used to hide her depression, disappointment, and fear. And his inferiority complex was identical to the one that made her question whether she really, truly believed that she deserved the fame and fortune of a great novelist.

His grandiose talk about plans and dreams and success were just that—words without action. They were both sabotaging their own success through the irresistible distractions of romance, criticism, anger, and sadness. And she realized that his no-show behavior mirrored her not showing up for herself to figure things out.

She also remembered what she'd read in Napoleon Hill's book, *Think and Grow Rich*: that most men don't achieve fame and fortune until they're in their forties because they're too busy in their twenties and thirties being slaves to sex. "Hill says if you channel your sexual power—the most powerful energy our bodies can create—into your dreams, then you can achieve phenomenal success. I realized, if I invest in myself and my career all the time, energy, and passion that I'm squandering on romance, I can win the Pulitzer Prize for literature!"

So staring into her lover's eyes, at that moment, Nina knew it was over. It was time to prune this golden apple from her relationship tree, so that she could cultivate stronger roots, mightier branches, and truly exotic fruits. "I need to focus on myself," Nina told her lover. "I need to figure out who I am and what I want."

And she left. Nina silently blessed him and this bittersweet experience, then released him. After that, she evaluated all the people in her life—and gently got to pruning!

"Soon as I wiped the slate clean and did the hard work of answering three important questions: 'Who am I? Why do I exist? Am I all that I'm capable of being?' " she says, "all these wonderful opportunities blossomed. Book deals, teaching college, speaking engagements, consulting jobs. It's amazing. Once I got real with myself, got my head out of the clouds and grounded my feet in reality, the authentic Nina showed up and knew exactly what she wanted."

Awesome new people, she says, began showing up, too. "I'm recasting the film of my life with phenomenal characters," she says.

"It's like when you're ready, the universe does a casting call and does the auditions for you. And they just come knocking."

Now Nina is thriving: writing books, teaching college, and speaking. For the past several years, she has been investing time and energy to turn within and connect with herself. She has been figuring out who she is, what she wants, and how she can best contribute to the world.

"I'm learning to trust Nina, believe in Nina, respect Nina, and stay committed to what Nina wants and needs. As a close friend once said, 'You can't *find* the right person, until you *become* the right person.' "

Amazingly, just when Nina fell in love with the new woman that she had become, she clicked with a wonderful man who reflected back all the positive qualities that she had been cultivating within herself. "It happened like magic," she says. "As soon as I announced to myself that 'I'm ready' for romance, it's like the Universe said, 'Your wish is my command!' This phenomenal man literally appeared. Now a thrilling, wholesome relationship is thriving and growing."

Nina's story exemplifies the power of pruning our relationship trees. She had the courage and discipline to remove a branch. She turned within to nurture her roots and her core. And that produced a brand new branch—a romantic relationship that is strong, healthy, and fruitful.

Ultimately, by releasing her lover, Nina was practicing Proverbs 22:24: "Abandon abusive friendships," because relationships that reinforce our negative beliefs abuse our chances for success. This, however, takes work and courage. We may keep toxic people in our lives out of a warped sense of loyalty or debt, and many of us fear the awkwardness or hostility that could result by breaking off a relationship. But by ending negative relationships now, you're freeing space to invite positive people into your life. So how do you start?

Evaluate How the People in Your Life Contribute to—or Detract from—Your Happiness, Productivity, and Prosperity

Does your "inner circle" reflect the type of person that you want to be? If not, you need to prune those individuals from your relationship tree. How? Start by thinking about the old saying, "Birds of a feather flock together." If you're flocking with birds who are going nowhere and doing nothing, then it's time to fly off with a better flock. Sociologists refer to the "birds of a feather" phenomenon as *homophily*—the tendency of people to associate and connect with people similar to themselves.

Shankar Vedantam writes in *The Washington Post*, "While there is nothing wrong with being around others who are similar to yourself, research sociologists, Lynn Smith-Lovin of Duke University and Mario Luis Small of the University of Chicago, said that people and organizations pay a price for homogeneity. In politics, for example, the fact that people rarely have friends with different views makes it difficult to seek common ground or to examine one's positions closely, therefore, I have no reason to challenge or question my own beliefs."

Researchers say homophily is on the rise because it is a natural tendency for us humans to surround ourselves with people who reflect who we are. So how can you determine whether homophily is causing you to waste precious time and energy on bad relationships?

Make a chart of the twelve closest people in your life. Evaluate their values, their lifestyles, their goals, their progress, and how you enhance their life versus how they enhance yours. Is it at least equal? Are you compromising or synergizing? Are you each adding value so that one plus one equals eleven instead of two?

Think about how these people are now, compared to when the relationship began. Are they still working as diligently as you are to climb the ladder of success? Or have they become lazy, discouraged, or jaded? Are they serving others or are they selfishly focused on themselves? Do you feel you're getting as much out of the relationship as the other person is? It should be even.

Have they picked up any bad or illegal habits such as excessive drinking, using drugs, or gambling? If so, how can you help them? Have they done anything to make you suspicious that perhaps they're taking advantage of your friendship?

As you'll see, some relationships are clearly ready for termination. Some are definitely keepers. But other folks—say, for example, a high-profile, lucrative client who's high maintenance and hard on the nerves—take some consideration. Most times in business, money talks, so it's about how to manage this relationship to stay sane and keep the client.

For anyone who clearly subtracts from your life, draw a red line through their name. If someone has equal good and bad points, make a detailed list of the relationship's pros and cons.

Don't Judge People by Their Relatives

One reason for aggressively developing a diverse array of good and productive friendships is because it's God's way of apologizing for our relatives.

We get our families in the random lottery of life called the "gene pool." Therefore we should never judge people based on their relatives. Unfortunately, many situations require us to be around parents, siblings, cousins, and others whose criticism, jealousy, and backstabbing cause misery every time. Try to avoid sustained interaction with them; if you must face them at a funeral, wedding, or holiday gathering, imagine yourself coated in Teflon so that nothing they say or do can stick. And remember this African proverb: "It is not what you call me, it is what I answer to."

My trick? Bless them and release them. You must deliver yourself from that evil and never look back.

End Toxic Relationships and Nurture Positive Ones

Now, what's the number one rule for ending relationships? Never burn bridges. One day you may need to return back over that bridge. But if it's charred and crumbling from your first crossing, you'll never be able to connect with the person on the other side.

Take Diana Ross and the Supremes. Their breakup, when Ross went solo, was notoriously ugly and bitter. So years later, in 2000, when Ross tried to lure founding member Mary Wilson to join her and two former Supremes in a concert tour, Wilson turned down the $4 million offer. And that left Ross and her duo with the impossible task of finding a singer who could recreate Wilson's talent and Supreme chemistry and fit. As a result, the tour was disastrous.

"It is not what you call me, it is what I answer to."

—African proverb

So how can you prune your relationship without burning bridges? Gracefully walk over that bridge, out of that person's life, without ever telling them that you're bidding them adieu. Adios.

How? Always exit a relationship on a high note. I typically express a good-bye by doing something for the person. It may be the last thing I do for them, but I end it with a smile and pleasant words. I never tell people, "This is the end of the relationship." Nor do I say, "Don't call me anymore, you crazy person. I never want to hear from you again." It's never that abrupt or abusive. If I end a relationship with you, you'll know it happened when you never hear from me again.

Sometimes a relationship takes a wrong turn because someone picks up a bad habit or is going through a challenge. Those are times when we need to "park" our relationships. We know they're there, but for the moment we don't need to be in touch. Watch this person from afar. Will they get back on track? Or continue their kamikaze flight? You may want to give them space to focus on their issue—whether it's grieving after the loss of a loved one, going through a divorce, or finding themselves, their voice, or their purpose.

Other times we park relationships because it's not convenient or appropriate to talk with that person more than a few times a year. I have 1,500 people in my industrial strength Rolodex. I'm not in touch with these people regularly in one form or another. Realistically, I have them in a sort of parking lot where I park my relationships and call on them when I need them or when I can add value to their lives. And they do the same with me. Not everybody wants to hear from you all the time. I know they're my friends and I can call on them. I know what they can and cannot do. And when a win-win opportunity comes along for both of us, I'll call and put the relationship back in gear.

Now what if someone burns you? What if their presence in your life turns toxic and they infect your personal and professional endeavors? What if they do something terrible that costs you money, time, and emotion? What if they insult you in a playful manner that deep down hurts you?

Your first obligation is to confront them in a way that's honest, direct, and tactful. You have to let them know what they did wrong and how it hurt you; they may not even be aware of it. Whether they agree or disagree, at least they know how you feel. Too many times folks embark on a whispering campaign, which makes everyone look bad. Remember what Eleanor Roosevelt said: "Great minds discuss ideas; average minds discuss events; small minds discuss people."

Sometimes, of course, we get so irate, we curse someone out. I don't recommend that. But it happens to everyone. People lob verbal bombs at each other or engage in one-upsmanship. We fear people who are oblivious to the damage of the hurtful language they use. And too often we lack the courage to confront that person about their unintended destructive behavior.

> *"Great minds discuss ideas; average minds discuss events; small minds discuss people."*
>
> —Eleanor Roosevelt

The best way to handle this—to mend or end a bad relationship—is to have a conversation. In person, on the phone, or—my favorite—in writing. That way, your letter serves as an official record of why you are terminating the relationship.

I'm famous for my tell-it-like-it-is letters. Again, I don't say, "This is the end of our relationship." Instead the letter serves as a formal, written way to express my concerns and dissatisfaction about whatever misunderstandings we had.

Then I bless it and I release it. And I basically learn the lessons and move on. I forget about the person and refuse to dwell on the issue. I don't stew in the toxic juices of what went wrong. In life you either win or you learn, so don't lose the lesson or you are bound to repeat it.

But here I'm talking about toxic people. Folks who stab a giant ice pick into your exuberant bubble as you put a hot new idea into action. So-called friends whose cynicism stings your cheeks as they question everything you do. Family members whose jealousy inspires vicious gossip.

What if the toxic relationship in your life is your boss? A neighbor? A relative with whom you come in contact every day? What if you think you "can't" end that relationship? Think about it this way: If you don't do it now, the relationship could end you, because science proves that anger, stress, and negativity can change our body chemistry to cause depression, heart attacks, and cancer. So if you allow someone to make your blood boil, they are poisoning your mind and body with toxic energy.

If you think you "can't" get away from this poisonous relationship now, you eventually will suffer the consequences with an ulcer, depression, or severe anxiety. Is it worth it? Absolutely not. No job or relationship is worth your life. Even if the toxic person is your spouse. Most of us get about seventy or eighty years here on Earth, if we're lucky, so why would we want to waste a single minute in misery?

I don't. I'm having too much fun doing what I do. But I'm disturbed by the frequency with which people ask me the "evil boss" question. They say they're in jobs they hate so much that they don't want to get up in the morning, but that they "can't" escape the misery.

You must deliver yourself from that evil. Get away from anybody who kills your vitality. Transfer to another department, take a sabbatical, start looking for another job. Use a bad situation to find a better one. This is a signal from Fate that you should evaluate where you are, how you got there, and where you want to go. They say God never shuts a window without opening a bigger, better door. So consider it a blessing in disguise that your boss is inspiring you to pinpoint your dreams and fly away.

As you do this, really get in touch with yourself. Too many of us are in unhappy situations because we did not get the college degree or the job we desired. We did what Mom and Dad wanted us to do. We succumbed to pressure from society that success means doctor, lawyer, or dentist, when true success comes by doing what makes us happy. In fact, it may take time to quiet those voices and actually figure out what we really want. That's okay. Take some quiet time to think about what would make you excited to get up and work every day.

Meanwhile, find a way to forgive the people who have hurt you. This enables you to release pain, anger, and disappointment so that it does not poison your current and future relationships. Then, once you've pruned the bad relationships from your life, you have more time and energy to nurture the positive ones and create new friendships.

> *"Associate with the happy and fortunate."*
>
> —author Robert Greene

This brings to mind Robert Greene's book, *The 48 Laws of Power*. Law #10 is "INFECTION: AVOID THE UNHAPPY AND UNLUCKY: You can die from someone else's misery—emotional states are as infectious as diseases. You may feel you are helping the drowning man but you are only precipitating your own disaster. The unfortunate sometimes draw misfortune on themselves; they will also draw it on you. Associate with the happy and fortunate instead."

Once you do the hard work of pruning the toxic branches from your relationship tree, new relationships will yield golden apples to nourish your life with happiness, fulfillment, and prosperity.

Exercise for Truth #5

Make a list of the twenty closest people in your life, including friends, family members, and business associates. Are they part of your personal, operational, or strategic network? Then rate how each person enhances your life by considering some of the following factors:

    Makes me happy
    Helps me prosper
    Provides advice, guidance
    Irritates me
    Costs me business
    Wastes my time
    Enhances my business
    Enhances my life
    Tells the truth
    Makes me feel valued
    Makes me feel used
    Inspires me
    Discourages me
    Makes me feel serene
    Makes me suspicious

Now evaluate what you've revealed about each person in your life. If you find that a friend or associate is making you feel bad, costing you business, or taking advantage of you, find a way to graciously end that relationship. For those who are enhancing your life, vow to strengthen those relationships by showing your appreciation for the positives that they contribute to your personal and professional endeavors. Know that when you prune the sickly branches from your relationship tree, you will strengthen the strong branches and make room for new relationships to grow.

Key CLICK Factors

Always

◆ Learn the lesson from every encounter so you do not have to repeat it.

◆ Keep your words both soft and tender, because tomorrow you may have to eat them.

◆ Point out people's strengths, not just their weaknesses.

Keep in Mind

◆ That we should be glad we don't get everything we ask for.

◆ That love, not time, heals all wounds. When you harbor bitterness, happiness docks elsewhere.

Do Not

◆ Seek revenge or justice. Rather, focus on grace and forgiveness.

◆ Think a person is perfect because you fell in love with him or her.

Make Sure To

◆ Surround yourself with people smarter than you; it's the easiest way to grow.

◆ Build relationships with a diverse array of people with varying skills, talents, insights, and experiences; everyone should not be like you.

◆ Forget about false hope, and confront the most difficult facts about an unproductive relationship.

Trust First; Distrust Must Be Earned

Trust—or the lack of it—is at the root of success or failure in relationships and in the bottom-line results of business, industry, education and government.

—Stephen Covey

TRUST IS THE bedrock of life, love, and every relationship. Period. It is the single most important factor in building personal and professional relationships; it is the cornerstone of relationships that fit and feel right. Without trust, we have nothing. "Trust implies accountability, predictability and reliability," writes leadership guru John Maxwell. Yet from an early age we are programmed to distrust; we are warned: "Don't talk to strangers." Now, as wary adults, it's counterintuitive and downright scary to see good in people first. So start within, by trusting yourself, then believe in the good of people—first.

Imagine a gorgeous, successful man and a beautiful, charismatic woman. With one glance, they click. But while their romance flourishes, they continue to attract aggressive admirers. How, then, does a couple maintain trust when it looks like temptation is lurking everywhere?

This is the vexing question in an otherwise fairy-tale love story for Veronica Conway. It's only vexing, says the forty-year-old professional coach in San Francisco, because her boyfriend sometimes views her through a lens of distrust.

"It's a tone, a way of asking questions—it feels a little like an interrogation," says Veronica. "It starts with the *why* question." And the trigger for the barrage of *whys* is usually another man.

"Men are very attracted to me," Veronica says. "My boyfriend, Robert, has some assumptions about when I'm out with him, or when men approach me. He gets kind of insecure about how they do that."

An example? The couple was at a reception when a man approached. Later, Robert asked, "Why did you introduce me to everyone in the room as your fiancé, but not with this guy?" Veronica's response: "Well, honey, I've dated him once or twice before and I wanted to let him down a little gently."

But Robert wasn't hearing that. He responded: "I should be the most important priority on your mind, not that man's feelings." Veronica says this dialogue is the breaking point for many couples. One accuses, the other defends, more hot buttons get pushed, and the argument gets nastier with each verbal swipe.

But, being a creative, innovative coach who counsels individuals and couples in relationships—and the daughter of a '60s revolutionary who taught her to think way outside the box—Veronica applies professional expertise to her personal life.

"We had to work through that," she says, adding that the problem is that her boyfriend comes to a situation with the assumption that every man will try to make a play at an attractive woman. And the issue of distrust arises when he questions how Veronica will respond when any random Casanova tries to cast his spell.

And that violates Truth #6. For Veronica and Robert, chemistry is unquestionably the attraction in their relationship. But, given this testy issue in their romance, how do they "fit"?

Veronica and Robert fit by coming to the relationship as two mature adults whose past experiences as individuals and as partners in previous romances have blessed them with the wisdom to know that they're right for each other. They fit because they're both ready to handle the pressures of a high-profile relationship as two successful, attractive people.

Perhaps a decade ago, neither would have had the trust, the confidence, or the maturity to thrive in such a relationship. But for them, right now, the chemistry, fit, and timing are perfect. And their fit is sufficiently tenacious to withstand Robert's mini-bouts of insecurity.

So how does Veronica keep *her* cool when a bevy of beauties bat their eyelashes at her man? "I'm brilliant at it," she says with a confident tone. "If you want to keep a man, create absolute freedom and space for who he is. That's why he's in love with me. I give him all the space in the world to be who he is."

Her calm confidence is all the more remarkable when she describes her "extremely gorgeous" boyfriend like this: "Six-foot-seven, chocolate brown skin, with beautiful high cheekbones and long eyelashes. He played college ball and has an athletic physique. He has a big, beautiful deep voice." Sounds like a woman's dream, right?

Right! "Women come into his presence and you can feel them faint inside," Veronica says, because Robert loves women. And his successful business ventures put him in the spotlight. "It's tangible. His approach is very loving and gentle. He's present and engaging and loving. And in all that masculinity, there's a real softness."

Veronica, who's divorced after a ten-year marriage, cops a rather clinical detachment: "He's an alpha male, and women want to be in the presence of an alpha male. So I let them have their moment. I trust him, so I don't have to worry about them."

But Veronica says the secret to her success—to never get jealous—is to understand that Robert's interactions with other women are not about *her*. They're about *him*—and the innocent pleasure one gets from interaction with the opposite sex.

"The more women get possessive," she says, "the more men get claustrophobic and they run. So women's possessiveness in a love relationship creates the opposite reaction."

If you're still not getting how Veronica can virtually shut off the mental jealousy button that vexes most men and women in passionate romances, take a listen to how she does it. "I trust him first," she says. How? She says she worked with an expert who trained her to explore her own sexual energy and to release any root causes of jealousy.

"It taught me to assign meanings to things in a new way," she says. "For Robert, the women are coming at him, he's going to respond, and *I ain't mad at him*. I totally understand why they're responding. If I'm going to pick a powerful man as a mate, I have to be okay with that."

Sadly, Veronica says, Robert's distrust and jealousy ultimately destroyed the relationship; they broke up.

The lesson? Consult with a professional to explore your ability to trust yourself and others. Then, if there's a block, work hard to dislodge it, to free yourself of that negative energy—so that you can learn to trust first. And that will invite infinite beauty and bounty to flow into your life.

That's how Veronica harnessed this extraordinary confidence, which is rooted in her hard work to find out who she is, what she wants, and how she can live to the best of her abilities.

In fact, it's the essence of Truth #6: *Start within, by trusting yourself, then believe in the good of people, first.*

Veronica lives this doctrine 24-7. "You can't trust another person until you fully trust yourself," she says. "It's an inside-out job." She says her clients experience an "Aha!" moment when they go inward and this idea illuminates their minds.

"The paradox is that once you fully trust yourself, you don't need to trust others," she says. "I don't worry about other people. I trust me and my instincts, I trust life, I trust my capacity to show up and meet the situation, to respond to whatever life brings. And that eliminates that whole, 'Do I trust you?' question."

So if you put Truth #6 into play in your life right now, you'll be able to experience Veronica's serenity when a lightning-bolt-from-the-sky moment occurs and you make that perfect connection. You can't plan it. Or look for it. Or advertise for it. You have to wait for the universe to deliver it, at the most unexpected moments.

For Veronica, she was at a jazz club with a male colleague when Robert walked in. "It felt like time stood still," she says, "like it was a glitch in the matrix. Everything around us seemed to stop. We weren't really saying anything, but the energy was so powerful. If you were in a five-foot space around us, you could feel what happened between us, it was that visceral." Visceral. Time-stopping. "I just knew, from the moment I saw him," Veronica says. "I just knew."

This inexplicable phenomenon (let's call it the alignment of chemistry and fit) that can occur with best friends, a mentor, a business partner, a great boss, or a spouse is the essence of a "click." And it inspires trust.

Yet when I tell people during speeches or in casual conversation to embrace the idea of trusting first, they often scowl as if I've asked them to swim with sharks or walk barefoot in the snow. That would make them feel exposed. Vulnerable. Reckless.

That's because our first instinct is to distrust until someone proves him- or herself worthy of our trust. And exposing ourselves to what we believe are the wicked ways of the world, lurking in strangers, is terrifying. Likewise, opening ourselves up to trust people in the competitive, ruthless business world may sound naïve or reckless—even though the opposite is true.

"Trust is the emotional bank account between two people that enables them to have a win-win performance agreement."

—Stephen Covey

I'm going to show you that by trusting first, we release negative energy that's actually holding us back from clicking—from building extraordinary relationships—and from living our most successful lives.

Think about it. The secret to success is connecting with people through relationships; without trust, you have no relationship. "Trust is the emotional bank account between two people that enables them to have a win-win performance agreement," Stephen Covey writes. "If two people trust each other . . . they can then enjoy clear communication, empathy, synergy and productive interdependency. If one is incompetent, training and development can help. But if one has a character flaw, he or she must make and keep promises to increase internal security, improve skills and rebuild relationships of trust."

That's why you should spend more than half your time—yes, upwards of 60 percent of your time—growing and nurturing your relationships. Research proves that very successful people invest that much time in cultivating, nurturing, and developing relationships at work, at home, and in the community. They are building trustworthy relationships for the long haul.

Granted, this is a gradual process. Yet it's extremely gratifying to throw off the cloak of suspicion that darkens our interactions with everyone we meet. When we stop always looking for the bad in people and instead look for the good, we can let our guard down and let life shower us with goodness.

And that starts with understanding what trust is. *Webster's New World Dictionary, Second College Edition* defines it as: *a firm belief or confidence in the honesty, integrity, reliability, justice, etc. of another person or thing; faith; reliance.*

Notice the word *faith.* Trusting is faith that things will work out. And if they don't, it's usually a blessing in disguise.

Oprah Winfrey calls this "sunrise faith"—having faith in yourself, your life, and your spiritual beliefs that's as strong as your belief that the sun will rise tomorrow. We don't question the dawn; we know it's coming in a matter of hours. We must apply that confidence to ourselves, our goals, and the spirit that guides us.

For many people, their strongest source of trust is their spiritual beliefs. When you trust that God or a higher power is guiding your life, then you're getting excellent practice at trusting in the goodness of life and goodwill of people, even strangers.

The problem lies in the fact that trust can be broken beyond repair in a split-second. We can easily betray someone's trust by lying, cheating, gossiping, breaking promises, being two-faced, and withholding important information. That's why trusting first is not for the faint of heart; it requires a keen sense of self, personal confidence, and established values.

I frequently refer to the wisdom of the great political and spiritual leader Mahatma Gandhi, who cited seven things that are perilous and destructive to humanity. I use these seven points to evaluate the trust factor in my short- and long-term relationships. They are:

- ◆ Wealth without work
- ◆ Pleasure without conscience
- ◆ Knowledge without character
- ◆ Commerce without morality
- ◆ Science without humanity
- ◆ Worship without sacrifice
- ◆ Politics without principle

I've established my own parameters and thresholds for measuring each of these things within each person I meet. Initially, I assume we are in sync. As time goes by, we become either closer or further apart. Thus, the time we spend together or the things we do together expands or contracts.

Here's an example. I often get calls from those who wish to convince me that they have a surefire way for me to earn $10,000 a week without having to do much work. Sometimes they even claim that they will do the work for me. My distrust flag goes up immediately. How often have you met those who believe in prayer without work? There are those politicians who will change to win instead of win to change. Have you met those who put profit before ethics? We must give everyone the benefit of the doubt, but you must eventually synchronize your values with the values of those with whom you will have a meaningful and productive relationship.

Strangers are just friends waiting to happen.

As the old saying goes, strangers are just friends waiting to happen. So how can you get to work on trusting?

Know Thyself

Ask yourself, "Who am I, why do I exist, and am I all that I am capable of being?"

Those are the simplest questions in life. And you'll spend your entire existence trying to answer them. That puts you miles ahead of most people, because they don't know to ask themselves these basic questions. As a result, they never seek the answers, and miss out on a fulfilling, purposeful life.

> *"If one is out of touch with oneself then one cannot touch others."*
>
> —Anne Morrow Lindbergh

The secret to a trusting and productive relationship that fits you is to figure out exactly who you are, why you're here, and how you can maximize your lifelong potential. Throughout this process, remember the words of writer Gloria Anzaldúa: "I change myself, I change the world."

And to change yourself, you have to understand "Who am I?" The answer lies in the Big Picture of your life: where and how you grew up, who influenced you—for better or for worse—and how those influences inspired you.

Did your experience as you nursed your ailing grandmother inspire you to become a geriatric nurse? Is your childhood fascination with playing "dress up" in elaborate costumes calling you to quit your corporate job and work in theater? Did your parents' paycheck-to-paycheck existence, and lack of money management skills, inspire you to learn financial planning to help others manage money? Perhaps your recent diagnosis with diabetes—after years of poisoning yourself with sugar and grease—is prompting you to educate parents and children to eat healthy and avoid this horrific epidemic.

Think about it: if you don't know who you are and what you want, and have no foundation of strong values, then you're vulnerable to those who want to tell you who you are. But when your Self is watertight, you're immune to the negative while focused strictly on the positive and prosperous.

Plus, this introspection will put you on track to figuring out "Why do I exist?" We are all here for a reason; it's up to us to find it and act on it. Be warned, though, it will take soul-searching and patience to pinpoint your passion and purpose, especially if you've been working for years in a trade that you despise. I always say, you're in the wrong profession if you can quit your job today and be happy.

> *"I change myself, I change the world."*
>
> —writer Gloria Anzaldúa

And too many people feel that way. In fact, 75 percent of workers are still on a quest to find their dream job, according to CareerBuilder.com. Unfortunately, fear keeps them stuck in jobs that bore or frustrate them; when the economy chokes and the employment market squeezes, people hold even tighter to their mind-numbing work for the financial stability and benefits. Yes, we have to feed our families and provide health insurance.

But the reality is, stability in today's work world is an illusion. A pink slip is just as likely to send a valued veteran who's been at the company for forty years packing as it is a young, enthusiastic new hire. That's why changing careers involves less risk than you think; the real risk lurks in dying with your dreams still inside. So it will be liberating and exhilarating to find a calling that you love so much, you would do it for free.

For me, that's speaking. For a writer friend of mine, it's writing. We love what we do so passionately that it doesn't feel like work. It's fun. It's thrilling. Every new experience excites us.

Find that, and it will be your greatest gift to yourself. Because once you're indulging your purpose and passion, everything else in your life will sparkle. And to keep it sparkling—as successful people know—You, Inc. must undergo an annual "Who am I?" audit. Whether it's your birthday, New Year's Eve, or the anniversary of your business, critique your strengths, weaknesses, actions, and accomplishments so that you may do even better next year.

This brutal self-assessment will answer: "Am I all that I am capable of being?" If the answer is no, get to work. Figure out what's holding you back. Bad habits, such as procrastination, lack of follow-up, or an inferiority complex can sound a death knell for your dreams. Identifying these obstacles is the first step toward moving them out of your way.

So take the answers to these questions and create the vision. Paint a mental picture of what that involves, a picture of yourself, your life, and the people you recruit to make it happen. Envision your ideal life in vivid detail: clients praising your work; friends thanking you for supporting them through a tough time; your family thriving and achieving health and happiness; yourself smiling with peace and prosperity.

Write it down by sketching word snapshots of the life you desire. Concentrate on those images every day; they will become a self-fulfilling prophecy! At the same time, believe and act as if You, Inc. is a Fortune 500 enterprise. And knowing the complete profile of You, Inc. will enable you to trust yourself—and others.

Listen to Your Intuition

That little voice inside your head, which speaks from visceral reactions in your gut and in your heart, holds infinite wisdom. So listen to it. Trust your inner voice to assess the people you meet. Remember Gandhi's seven things that could destroy you.

Are you trained to trust your own intuition? Some people call it a sixth sense, or a hunch. It's the same little voice in your head telling you not to walk into that dark parking garage alone—and then you find out the next day someone was robbed there. That same voice is talking to you about the people you meet.

Listen to it, trust it. It can feel when someone has bad karma. Some people simply have a bad vibe. Period. They attract gloom and doom; they radiate anger and hostility. And they don't belong anywhere on your team.

So, if, upon first handshake, you hear *This is a bad person*, then heed that warning. If the voice within says, *This person makes me feel happy and inspired*, then consider that person trustworthy.

Observe people. If a prospective client degrades the waiter over your first business lunch, let that serve as a warning about how he or she treats people—and possibly you, too, if the deal sours. If someone tries to entice you into unscrupulous activities—or boasts about his own—question whether he approaches friendships and business relationships with the same sneakiness.

Pay attention to a person's eyes, body language, speech patterns, and energy or vibe. All this can push them up or down the scales of trust. So let everybody start at the top of the scale. If they say or do something that makes them slip downward, act accordingly.

In a *Time* magazine article about the brain, science writer J. Madeleine Nash writes about "mirror neurons." Those are nerve cells in the brain that fire when you initiate an action or when you perceive an action imitated by others, triggering a sympathetic response. "They operate on a subconscious level; their activity is reflexive and involuntary. Yet their firing patterns may be capable of encoding not just movements but also the meaning behind the movements." Interestingly, Nash writes that your brain and my brain and our neighbor's brain engage this "mirror system" in a slightly different way, allowing us to respond to each individual that we meet in a unique fashion.

For me, this scientific insight explains why we click with some people, yet we feel no connection with many other men and women we encounter. Our brains literally respond differently to each person we meet.

From there, the question that I frequently hear is, "Now that we've clicked, how do we establish trust? What is the basis for trust? How do you know you can trust someone?"

My answer: find common ground, common bonds, values, and goals. Perhaps you know someone in common; that "friend of yours is a friend of mine" endorsement can provide a character reference that brings innate trust to the relationship.

I also recommend that you evaluate a person by their deeds, not just their words. This requires patience, because it takes time to share experiences and observe how this new person acts and makes you feel. The reward lies in discovering vast common ground, where trust can flourish and deepen.

As you're evaluating a new person's trust factor, take a hard look at whether he or she trusts others. That can be a red flag—a red flare, even—to steer clear of a miserable soul. Because people who say they "trust no one" are doomed to emptiness and lack.

Many times, extreme distrust is rooted in the pain of getting burned by people you loved and admired, or those you hired to do an important job. But we cannot allow those unscrupulous men and women to poison our faith in people. We must release the sting of betrayal and trust again. Otherwise, it is impossible to "click" and build powerful relationships.

You'll understand this once you've dealt with people who refuse to trust. Their negative energy engulfs the entire room like a toxic cloud. Cynicism and suspicion tinge their every sentence. Their body language—crossing their arms, not making eye contact, scowling—creates a physical barrier.

And doing business with them is misery. They're not open or flexible. You have to explain and prove everything, and they still challenge every minuscule point. Why? Because they don't believe you. They don't trust you. And that turns you off, makes you take your friendship or business deal to someone else, someone who is pleasant and trustworthy.

If we don't get this one right, nothing else will matter. I am successful in my dealing with people because I inherently trust people. I take them for their word.

Have I been burned? Oh, yes. But what I've gained as a result has been far greater than whatever I've lost. Have I been mistaken or lied to? Of course. Have people said they can do something and can't? Yes, absolutely. But the ratio of getting burned to enjoying fabulous relationships inspires me to trust first.

Let Someone Earn Your Distrust by Giving Them the Benefit of the Doubt

Try giving strangers the benefit of trust as long as their actions prove worthy. Get down to business by following up on promises made, plans discussed, visions shared. Hold nothing back.

Applaud and appreciate people. The great author, leader, and speaker John Maxwell says in *25 Ways to Win with People*, "Believe the best about people, see things from their perspective, give them the benefit of the doubt and remember the good day, not their bad ones." Cheer them on when they say they've just become a CPA or a celebrated pianist or a volunteer in their daughter's classroom.

Resist the urge to hunt for proof that they're lying. That often comes out in suspicious statements such as: "I can't believe you honestly find time to work out six days a week with your heavy workload!" That puts the person in defense mode and casts negativity over the whole exchange; your skepticism could cost you a wonderful connection.

Instead, how about a congratulatory, "Wow, that's excellent!" Your positive response will elicit a smile; they will remember you for that.

We must switch our brain's default setting from distrust and reprogram it to trust first. The feminist writer Gloria Steinem said: "The first problem for all of us is not to learn but to unlearn." You can do that when you:

- **Believe what people say.** Proverbs 19:1 tells us: "Insist on integrity." And what is integrity but truthfulness, doing what you say you are going to do. I demand this of myself and I expect it from others. Expect good and good usually follows. Of course, don't be naïve; get résumés, referrals, and documentation that hopefully will serve more for recordkeeping than confirmation of one's credentials.

- **Don't worry about people's motives.** I have a friend who says she's suspicious of people because "everybody has an agenda." I remind her: "So do you!" But when we're living our most successful lives, my agenda meshes with your agenda so that we can win together! When we first meet, I engage you in conversation about yourself so I can find out who you are, what you want, what are your dreams. All the while, I'm flipping through my mental Rolodex to find someone or something to help you.

  Many times, however, our offers arouse suspicion: "Oh, you're giving me this. What do you want from me in return?" Sometimes I don't want anything right now. I just want you to have it because you need it. One day I may call on you for a favor. Or I may never call. But someone may ask you about me someday, and you'll have good things to say. These random acts of kindness with strangers are simple, yet they encourage a powerful spirit of trust. They also build a different kind of life insurance: even if someone speaks maliciously about you, your actions and your reputation will prove them wrong.

This is a secret that master connectors cherish—trust secures connections.

Exercise for Truth #6

We live in a scary, distrustful world. We live in a world full of happy, helpful people. Which is your outlook? I challenge you to believe in the goodness of people, first, and only cast out suspicion when it's provoked. To do that, you have to challenge yourself about why you're distrustful. Have you been burned in a business deal? If so, you must stop believing that everyone has the ill intentions of the person who burned you. Did your spouse have an affair that caused a painful divorce? If so, it's imperative that you believe that many honest, faithful people live in our world—and they're praying to connect with a wholesome person like yourself. But that can only happen if you're open to trusting in the goodness of people.

To cultivate a more trusting mind-set, coin a mantra that you can repeat throughout the day, especially when you encounter situations that tend to spark your distrust. Tell yourself, "I trust first." Or "I believe in the goodness of people." Or "I am attracting honest people." And "I believe what people say."

Also, remind yourself of situations in which you were tempted to distrust—only to learn later that the people involved were being honest and were in fact trustworthy. Dwell on those situations as proof that you can trust people and click your way into awesome relationships.

Key **CLICK** Factors

Always
- Have an open and honest agenda that includes something for the other person.
- See the strengths, not the limitations, in others.
- Search for ways to make others look good.
- Tend to the needs of others first.

Keep in Mind
- That great love and great achievements involve great risk. Don't lie to people to feed their ego. It's not about you. It's about the people around you, so stop trying to impress people. Be natural and spontaneous.

Do Not
- Judge people by their relatives. They didn't pick them. Judge them by their friends.
- Laugh at a person's dreams. People who don't have dreams don't have much.

Make Sure To
- Respect people for what they have done and from where they have come.
- Always add value and bring something to the table first.
- Give people your full attention by listening patiently without interruption.

Tailor Your Relationships for the Perfect Fit

When you stop worrying so much about yourself and start looking at others and what they desire, you build a bridge to other people, and you become the kind of person others want to be around. These are the keys to connecting.

—John Maxwell, author of *Connecting with People*

WE CONNECT WITH people with the holistic goal of helping others. In order to connect on a deep level, we must recognize that every interaction between two people is personal—even in business relationships. And the best way to personalize those relationships is to follow the Platinum Rule: treat others as *they* wish to be treated! This is based on the book *The Platinum Rule: Discover the Four Basic Business Personalities and How They Can Lead You* *to Success* by Tony Alessandra and Michael J. O'Connor. Find out what makes others happy, what makes them feel valued and appreciated. Then tailor your relationship to create a perfect fit.

A private jet. Chauffeured cars. An international deal in Europe. And an important lesson learned on the make-or-break nuances of business etiquette. Such were the elements of an "Aha!" moment that reminded Craig Callé of that valuable Platinum Rule.

It happened in the luxurious lobby of a prestigious hotel in Edinburgh, Scotland. That's where Callé—then a senior finance executive at an international company—was waiting for his CEO. The two men and several other associates were scheduled to ride in chauffeured cars to a Gulfstream 5 jet, which would take them to a meeting in another city.

"The CEO said we'd leave at seven," says Craig, who normally traveled alongside the CEO. "I was probably a minute or two late, at 7:02. It was the sort of thing in which an elevator stopping at one too many floors could make you a minute or two late."

But when Craig arrived in the richly appointed lobby to enter the chauffeured car with the CEO, the CEO was gone. Though surprised, Craig did not panic. Since they had a large group, a second car was waiting to transport him and the others to the jet, which would not leave until everyone arrived.

Although he played it cool on the outside—and the CEO never mentioned it—Craig says getting left behind inspired him to tailor his timing to the CEO's fast-forward approach to scheduling.

"I became conditioned to taking whatever time he said and subtracting ten minutes from it to accommodate his style," Craig says. "The CEO was very prompt. When he said seven, he meant ten of seven. While small and even trivial to others at the time, it was something that I noticed as an unwritten style that I incorporated into our relationship."

Craig says he's not even sure if the CEO noticed his assistant's absence in the car en route to the jet. So it wasn't like the CEO was trying to make a point such as, "Dammit, I'm going to leave!" It was more subtle, Craig says. The situation taught him that if he wanted to keep his respectful place at the top, then he'd better adjust himself to the unique and unspoken codes of conduct of his superiors.

In other words, Craig realized that in order to "fit" with perfect precision into the position that he cherished alongside the CEO, he would have to tailor his behavior to his boss's personal code of conduct. With meticulous attention to detail, Craig succeeded in doing that. Clearly, a person who is always running late would not fit into the CEO's world of being habitually early. In addition, it was only through Craig's careful study of his boss that he learned to put this Truth to work: treating the CEO as the CEO wishes to be treated—with extraordinary mindfulness of every valuable minute of his business day.

Thus, Craig skillfully endeared himself to his boss because he mastered the art of using chemistry, fit, and timing to craft win-win relationships in the business world. Chemistry opened the door for the relationship; Craig's efforts to fit into the CEO's style secured his position; and the timing of their partnership was ideal for both of them.

As you can see, putting chemistry, fit, and timing to work for you is all about your observations of other people's likes and dislikes, then putting Truth #7 to work by figuring out how you can treat them as they wish to be treated.

And, as Craig illustrated, these dynamics often play out with subtlety and nuance that can be easily overlooked. "It wouldn't get me fired, but it was important to him," Craig says. And that meant everything at the time.

Craig's meticulous attention to detail in relationships and the business that follows are his trademark for success. In fact, that's what impressed me when he contacted me in his new job as CEO of an online technology company to offer his software to my online networking organization, FraserNet.

My first connection with Craig in his sparse San Francisco offices was subtle. His starched dress shirt, handsome tie, and dark pinstriped suit mirrored my taste in business attire. He presented the right image; his confidence level was high, and his words and ideas flowed easily and quickly. In addition, I was impressed by his technology that is based on people first finding "common ground" to establish trust, a concept in sync with my own networking research and ideas. His in-depth knowledge of my business, his respect for my time, and his motherly attention to my creative comforts (coffee, lunch snacks, phone breaks) made me feel welcome, comfortable, and understood.

We immediately clicked because we speak a similar vocabulary. Several telephone conversations and e-mail exchanges proved that Craig's impeccable work style—and his keen knowledge of high-tech techniques for streamlining FraserNet's communications—would create a triple-win situation—for him, for me, and for our customers. And so we started doing business together. Today, when you click onto FraserNet.com, you see the result of our partnership: a co-branded version of his technology for our members.

Now, I want you to understand why I chose to do business with Craig, as opposed to the dozens of other technology communications experts who could have provided a similar service. The short answer? We connected. Craig and I connected quickly and easily—in three different ways—that made me like him and trust him.

How? Craig tailored our relationship for a perfect fit. He observed me, then customized the way he treated me based on my preferences for how I want to be treated. Plain and simple, he put Truth #7 to work, and it did.

First, Craig was a patient listener. He was also very thorough in his explanation of the technology that he was trying to get me to use. I confess, I am no computer whiz. I needed someone who could explain—twelve times over—how his product would work for me. Well, Craig explained it about fifteen times, with kindness and empathy.

At that moment, I felt impressed by his communication style. He fortified our new business relationship by spending the time and energy to show he wasn't just trying to make a buck; he truly cared that I would invest in his services as a well-informed and enthusiastic customer.

His behavior sharply contrasted with too many other people I've met in business. I'm talking about people who are impatient and myopic. They're so busy trying to sell you the features of their product, which they repeat over and over again, that they overlook your needs and how their product would add value to your goals. At the same time, they're so anxious to impress you by boasting of their accomplishments and accolades that they blow the deal, because you've figured out the deal is about what they want *from* you, not *for* you. This is where they fail.

And this is where people like Craig Callé succeed. Craig exhibited the traits of a master networker. In fact, he shared some insights that—even though I'm already an expert on the subject—enhanced my outlook on networking!

He verbalized a dimension of networking that, while I knew it existed, I had not put into words. He was the one who said to me that all great networking is based on the common ground of people, places, and things. And the more common ground you have with someone, the higher the trust level. And the higher the trust level, the more a person is likely to share key contacts, resources, and information.

As we proceeded to do business together that benefited both of us, Craig exemplified many of the Truths in this book. And as someone who joined my team, he proved that it's important to recruit people who are as smart as you or smarter, so that they bring to your table creativity and fresh ideas that help everyone prosper.

He also added value to my life purpose and my company. He gave me a point of view that I thought was valuable and useful. That viewpoint helped crystallize the point of this book: that in order to enjoy and maximize the full potential of networking, we must start thinking about connecting on a much deeper level.

Craig's long-term success proves the power of Truth #7. Nurturing relationships by treating others as they wish to be treated can bear glorious fruit for years to come. This lesson is most important for folks who do the opposite of Truth #7. They play the "assume" game. Do you?

Don't Assume

Think about it: if you ever start conversations with "I assume . . ." then the answer is yes. But that's not the way to win in relationships.

Do you say things such as "I assume you love chocolate"? Or "I assume we'll meet at your office"? Or "I assume that morning is your most creative time"?

Do you think in assumptions? For example, if an annual event was held at a particular venue one year, and you *assume* it will be there this year as well (so you don't check the brochure to confirm), you would be late or even miss the event entirely if you went to the wrong place.

Do you act on assumptions? For instance, do you assume that your business partner will agree to your idea to spend $15,000 on new computer equipment?

If you play the assume game, you may be losing out on wonderful new connections. Let's take time out and consider what my friend told me about her first day in journalism school. The professors admonished: "Never assume. It makes an *ass* out of *u* and *me*."

Think about that. The next time you hear someone say "I assume" and you realize their assumption is just plain wrong, you'll understand what I'm saying.

If you assume that your new client Sherry will love your favorite seafood restaurant, and you don't ask what she likes, you'll be embarrassed when you sit down and she cannot order anything because she's allergic to shellfish. In fact, the very smell of the crab legs and shrimp that you love could be deadly for her! Not a great way to click!

The problem? Guessing. When we assume what another person likes or wants, we are guessing. And guessing leaves far too much room for error.

Successful people operate on facts, not guesses. And because the variables in our lives are constantly in flux, it's important to think of those "facts" as "probabilities." For example, since John has been dieting for the past six months, he'll probably want to lunch with you at his favorite salad place. However, there's a chance he may be in the mood to indulge today—so he might want to blow his diet and chow down on pizza instead.

For you, as you tailor the relationship to each individual, your job is to remove the guesswork from the game—by asking questions to stay up-to-date on the person's likes and loves. When you cater to those, you strengthen the relationship by making them feel valued and appreciated.

Oh, and if you're worried about getting too personal, relax. Because every relationship is personal. Even business relationships. Especially business relationships. We do business with people we like. If I have a choice between doing a deal with you and doing a deal with a person who's rude, distrustful, and negative, I am going to choose you because you're polite and kind, and you make me feel appreciated.

Whether we're negotiating or taking bids for a contract or networking at a conference, we're interacting with people. And as people we're sensitive to how others treat us. Some of us have thicker skins than others. But we all have a heart that is vulnerable to love and loathing. So it's impossible to separate the personal from the professional. That's why, in order to excel in the professional arena, we must cultivate the personal. Here's how.

Always Ask, Never Stereotype

Whether or not it's true, this story that circulates regularly on the Internet is a poignant example of just how humiliating, hurtful, and even hilarious we can be when we stereotype.

Imagine a woman on vacation at a casino-hotel in Atlantic City. After collecting a big win at the slot machines, she decides to stow her treasure in her room before going to dinner with her husband. So she carries her heavy bucket of winnings to the elevator. When the doors open, she comes face-to-face with two black men—one of whom is tall and quite intimidating.

Fear paralyzes the woman for a moment, until she admonishes herself for assuming that just because the men are black they will harm her. The default button in her brain—that had her thinking in negative stereotypes about African American men—makes her feel ashamed. Still, she feels jittery about being alone in the elevator with them and her winnings.

Her cheeks burn with embarrassment. She's sure the men can read her mind, as if her horrible thoughts are flashing across her forehead like the television news crawl on the bottom of the screen on CNN.

Determined to act with courage, the woman forces her feet to step, one after the other, toward the two black men in the elevator. She positions herself with her back to the men, her face to the elevator doors as they close. Whew! She can avoid eye contact this way; the men will never know just how flustered she feels.

Time seems to stand still. Because the elevator does not move.

The woman's heart hammers. Is she now stuck with her money and these two men? Is this a setup? Are they going to rob her now? Sweat prickles under her clothes; her throat tightens with terror.

"Hit the floor," one of the men says.

The woman throws herself onto the floor. Quarters spray up, then rain down in a loud, dizzying clatter. She prays: *"Take my money and spare me."* The elevator feels terrifyingly still and silent.

"Ma'am," one of the men says, as if restraining himself from busting out with laughter, "if you'll just tell us what floor you're going to, we'll push the button."

The woman slowly raises her head. She looks at the men. One of them offers a hand to help her up. She feels dazed as the average-sized man says: "When I told my friend here to hit the floor, I meant that he should hit the elevator button for our floor," he says, biting his lip to stifle laughter. "I didn't mean for you to hit the floor, ma'am."

The woman aches with humiliation. Her heart urges her to apologize; her mouth is too stunned and ashamed to form words.

The clang of coins punctuates her awkward silence as the men help her collect the coins.

Ding! The elevator opens onto her floor. The men walk her to her room because she feels wobbly. "Good evening," they say outside her door.

As soon as she closes the door, she hears them explode in a fit of laughter. Stunned by the experience, the woman primps for dinner, then joins her husband downstairs.

The next morning, a dozen roses arrive at her room. One crisp hundred dollar bill waves from each flower. The card reads: "Thanks for the best laugh we've had in years." And it's signed by Eddie Murphy and Michael Jordan.

The lesson here? Never prejudge people—no matter their dress, culture, gender, age, race, or sexual orientation. I simply treat people as they wish to be treated, without prejudgment. Who are we to judge a person based on anything but their actions and deeds?

Finding out and assisting a person in fulfilling their unique purpose—without stereotyping—is a surefire way to connect, then click. Said simply: it is the best way to tailor your relationships for a perfect fit.

Take, for example, my friend who says chocolate makes her sick. To a chocolate lover, that's hard to fathom. But it's the truth. So now I know, when I'm sending her a token of my appreciation for a referral or a job well done, I do not send a box of Godiva. I send a fruit basket. Why? Because when I asked her what she loved, she pointed to the silver bowl of fresh fruit on her desk and said, "I snack on it all day long. Keeps my energy up."

Had I assumed that she, like most people, loves chocolate, I would have wasted my money and she would have not enjoyed the gift. In fact, my assumption might even have annoyed her. That's why I always ask people, "How do you prefer to be treated?"

My journalism friend says her professors had a warning about this as well: The only stupid question is the one you *don't* ask, because guessing gets you in trouble.

So don't be shy. Other people will be flattered that you're interested in their tastes and preferences. They will be touched that you're curious about what makes them feel valued and appreciated.

You can start with the old-fashioned *please* and *thank you*. In the laser-beam pace of our high-tech world, too many folks are forgetting to express gratitude and politesse. Write a thank-you note after an interview, a pleasant exchange at a business function, or receipt of that recommendation letter the CEO wrote for you. Include a small gift—a pen, an inspirational book, flowers (after you find out what he or she likes!)—to show that you appreciate the time and attention the person lavished on you. Showing gratitude and graciousness can only enhance your connections.

Ask, thank, and offer in every conversation. That's as simple as: "Thank you so much. Now what can I do to help you?"

One way to help every interaction is to block out the technological interruptions that bombard us around the clock. That means that when you're talking with a friend or client face-to-face, turn off your cell phone, Blackberry, pager, iPod, and any other electronic device. If you must keep it on vibrate, or if you absolutely have to answer, be careful how you respond. I often hear folks glance at the caller ID and say, "What does *she* want? I'll ring her back later." The person thought they were making me feel important, but it really made me wonder if they treat *my* calls that way when they're with someone else.

If you're expecting an important call that can't wait, politely inform the person you're with, in advance: "I'm sorry, but my accountant is on a deadline with the IRS and she has to run some numbers past me by eleven o'clock. I'll have to take her call."

I can't tell you how many times I've been in meetings where a colleague sets his phone and PDA on the table between us. Recently, a short meeting was constantly interrupted by the ringing, vibrating, and flashing of his gadgets. And every time, he answered or typed something back. That made me feel that he did not value me or my time. It irritated me that his attention was scattered between me and all of the people who were phoning and text-messaging him. Rather than tailor his behavior to make me feel valued, he was tearing apart our connection. As a result, I chose not to do business with him.

One of the best ways to tailor your relationship with anyone is to indulge them with the courtesy of your undivided attention. That means turning off all electronics, then checking messages and returning calls on your own time.

Observe People's Behavior, Expressions, and Body Language

Another way to find out what people like is to simply pay attention. If you're at a business breakfast and you notice that a potential client takes extra time to choose from the selection of herbal teas, that's your clue. Pay attention to what type he picks. Get him talking about tea—when he drinks it, what flavor he loves, how he developed this passion, how it makes him feel, and what rituals he has around his tea. Then you'll know that for your next meeting, you can say, "Let's talk about it over tea." Better yet, send him a gift basket of teas and accessories or a teacup with your company logo on it or a gift certificate for the local gourmet tea store. In the end, he will be delighted that you were so perceptive as to figure out what he loves. And he never knew you were "interviewing" him with the goal of tailoring your relationship to create a perfect fit.

Here's where listening is vital. Say you're making a connection with an architect whom you may hire to design your company's headquarters. In her office, she's listening to the Chicago Symphony Orchestra. Ask her about the music—her favorite instruments, symphonies, etc. Now you know, when it's time to thank her for a job well done, you can send her tickets to see the CSO when it comes to town.

Another example? A lunch date I had once with a man I used to work with. He was professional and golden-hearted. But when he took out his wallet—it wasn't even a wallet! It was a rubber band around credit cards, tattered business cards, and cash. Turns out his old wallet had ripped and he'd been too busy to replace it. So I did. I went to the store and bought him a sleek, black leather bifold. He was thrilled! His wife was amused, too.

When you start doing this, you'll love watching people's reactions to your usual attention to detail and random acts of kindness. Since most people do not pay attention to our individual likes and dislikes, you will really stand out and make a wonderful impression when you appreciate their uniqueness.

Jot Down Notes About a Person's Preferences, Favorites, Birthdays, Family Members, and Hobbies

When you meet someone new and you click, write on the back of his business card where you met. Include details that show common bonds: "belongs to my fitness club" or "collects rare coins" or "son goes to my daughter's school" and "wife loves lemon meringue pie." As the connection develops, you could even keep a file on this person. Keep track of his birthday, his alma mater, his health restrictions, his food preferences (favorite restaurant), and his wedding anniversary.

Jot down the names of his spouse and children; favorite hobbies and sports; on-going challenges (parent with Alzheimer's, physical therapy for racquetball injury, allergy to bee stings); favorite color; and anything else that may allow you to tailor your product or service to his tastes.

Knowing intimate facts about your associate enables you to lavish the relationship with a personal touch that is endearing and unforgettable. And as you customize your bond, you're building trust, enthusiasm, and a mutual, long-term desire to collaborate on exciting endeavors.

And it lets you in on a secret that all master connectors share: you must continue to help others to make important connections. Say you know Sam, who owns a graphic design business. You have a friend Julie, who's opening a new company that will need business cards and brochures. So you introduce Sam and Julie; Julie decides to do business with Sam. He does an excellent job; she's so thrilled that she sends him lots of referrals. This is a triple-win situation. Sam and Julie are thriving in business, and they're both loving you for making the connection that's blossoming on many levels. As a result, they will be more than happy to send referrals, services, and exciting new people your way in ongoing gratitude for the simple act of your introduction.

When I meet new people, my brain is constantly ticking down a list of the folks I know and the services they provide. You say you need a new accountant? I know the perfect person. You're moving to Phoenix? Oh here's my good friend's number. He loves to show new people around town. Your son is going to college in New

York? Here, have him call my sister so he can get a home-cooked Sunday dinner once in a while.

The more new connections you make for other people, the more good fortune will sparkle back on you. They will never forget how you spent your time and energy to introduce them to people who become part of their dream teams. And they will for many years express thanks by reciprocating your goodwill. In the end, their success is your success.

This deepens the connection by making them feel that you're investing in them and your future relationship. And when we elicit that in other people, they become willing to open up to us in friendship and in business. Again, as the Bible says, we have to give before we can get. And we find that in giving, we receive the most fulfillment in making others feel happy—by treating them the way they wish to be treated.

The folks at Cook Ross, Inc. (www.cookross.com), a company specializing in addressing the challenges of an increasingly diverse workplace, have produced a tremendously effective *Cultural Communication Guide* (*CCG*) that I have used very often in my travels around the world. I recommend that you pick it up and apply its wisdom to help you click with people whose cultural backgrounds differ dramatically from your own. When you find new ways to tailor your relationships across ethnic boundaries, you invite phenomenal new experiences to enhance your life on every level.

Exercise for Truth #7

This Truth requires you to do your research and be very observant. You essentially need to study people to learn their habits, their likes, their dislikes, their pet peeves, and their beliefs. Armed with that information, you can treat them accordingly—and click magically! Here are some traits to evaluate:

- **Favorite foods.** You'll know to invite your client to an Indian restaurant when you learn that it's her favorite cuisine. You'll know not to take her to a steakhouse when you find out she's a vegetarian.
- **Religious beliefs.** You'll know not to invite your friend to play golf on a particular day that happens to be the Sabbath or a holiday for his religion. You'll know not to invite your Muslim friend out to lunch during Ramadan, when his religious beliefs inspire him to fast.
- **Health.** If you're driving a client to a meeting, and you know that she's allergic to cigarette smoke, you will make arrangements to take a vehicle other than your own, in which you and your spouse routinely smoke. When you're hosting a lunch at your office, you'll serve salads with grilled chicken and fruit to clients who are health-conscious.
- **Hobbies.** When you discover that your new business associate enjoys boating, you'll know to hold your next lunch meeting on the restaurant-yacht that sails on your town's river. And when you find out that a member of your dream team loves to read, you'll celebrate his birthday with a gift certificate to his favorite bookstore.

The key to success in treating others as they wish to be treated is paying attention to what they say and do and asking questions. When you click, and you care deeply about bonding with another person, this will not feel like work. It will come naturally, and it will feel like a celebration of every wonderful person in your life. Enjoy!

Key **CLICK** Factors

Always

◆ Let people know you appreciate and need them, that whatever they bring to the table—big or small—is valuable in the total scheme of things.

◆ Ask, listen, and observe their response. Avoid a mismatch or conflict in values, and you will reduce the stress in the relationship.

Keep in Mind

◆ Giving credit is like a boomerang; toss it sincerely and freely and it will always come back to you. It if doesn't fit, don't force it; you are not compatible with everyone.

◆ Every person is your superior in some way; everyone has something to teach you.

◆ Money doesn't buy you class, so treat people accordingly.

Do Not

◆ Prejudge people based on color, class, age, gender, or physical handicaps.

◆ Focus on a person's weakness—talk about their gifts and strengths.

Make Sure To

◆ Respect people for what they have done and where they come from.

◆ Be sincere and genuine in your praise, recognition, and accolades; people can smell bull%$@# from 100 yards away.

◆ Add the value they want, not the value you want them to have.

PART 3

TIMING

Timing *noun*
1. a synchronizing of the various parts
2. the control of speed in order that it may reach its maximum at the proper moment
3. selecting the best time or speed for doing something to achieve maximum result
4. precise synchronization

Adapted from the *Random House Unabridged Dictionary*, © Random House, Inc., 2006.

f excellent chemistry and a great fit enable you to click with someone new, a thrilling new relationship awaits—if the timing is right.

Say you meet someone who shares your vision for a unique business—but he's leaving next week on a yearlong mission in South America. Or you sizzle in an electrifying encounter with an enchanting stranger—only to learn that he or she is getting married next week. Or the boss that you impressed years ago calls to offer an incredible job—a month before your first baby is due. In those situations, the timing is just plain bad.

When the timing is good, however, magic can happen in your relationships. If the business visionary just returned from his mission and is looking for an exciting new enterprise . . . and the sexy stranger just got divorced . . . and the job offer comes the day your child starts grade school . . . then the timing is perfect. And perfect timing allows us to truly click!

Truth #8: Make Peace, Not War, with Words, Truth #9: Be Open to Everything and Attached to Nothing; the Best Idea Wins, and Truth #10: It Takes Teamwork to Make the Dream Work reveal how to synchronize timing to spark and build fulfilling, prosperous relationships.

And how do you express that you're in sync with another person? By speaking. That's why Truth #8 urges you to make peace, not war, with words. When you choose your words carefully, you can speak your way into someone's heart, and you can seal the perfect business deal.

But if you allow vicious, angry words to shoot from your mouth, you can slay personal and professional relationships alike. That's why diplomacy—whether you're enraged, disappointed, or frustrated—is the ultimate rule number one for your communications with everyone. Because spoken words can never be taken back, they can fester in a person's mind for life.

And as you become a diplomatic wordsmith, you can further cultivate excellent timing with Truth #9. By being open to everything, attached to nothing, and letting the best ideas win, you are inviting new ideas and energy to make magic in your life. This openness attracts innovation and unique opportunities. And your ability to release old thoughts and habits enables you to embrace exciting new concepts and practices. As a result, you'll click with equally progressive people who can reward you with friendships and prosperity.

These new connections are the core of Truth #10: know who's on your side. For starters, be on your own side. You must love yourself, adore what you're doing with your life, and feel thrilled about your place in the world—before you can deeply click with others. Only then can you build a team to make your dream come true.

And teamwork makes the dream work! By putting all of these Truths to work to create perfect chemistry, fit, and timing, you can "click" your way into a phenomenally fulfilling and prosperous life that will shower you with infinite thrills and riches.

Ways to Enhance Timing

◆ Be observant
◆ Look for opportunity
◆ Be creative
◆ Be flexible
◆ Anticipate
◆ Be persistent

Make Peace, Not War, with Words

Restraint: look it up if you don't know what it means. For my purposes, it means stopping yourself from doing or saying something that might come back to hurt you or someone else. It is exercising control or moderation. It is pulling back when your impulse is to push forward. It doesn't mean you can't act with your heart, but you have to make sure your head is in the right place.

—Montel Williams in his book *Life Lessons*

OUR MOUTH IS one of the most violent weapons that we bring to the battlefield of life. Words have power! But we can create win-win situations for you, me, and others by mastering the art of constructive critique and empowerment; when we make our words as accurate and as penetrating as the surgical precision of a scalpel, we can prevent bloodshed and scarring. Instead, we repair damage, teach, heal, and inspire.

When respected colleagues anger Hattie Hill with an obnoxious request, she does not lash back with criticism or rage. Instead, this maven of international business has mastered the art of verbal feedback with stealth, diplomacy, and style, so that the offenders never know what hit them. But they hear her disapproving silence loud and clear.

How? She plays humble, then quickly changes the subject. "I don't even have to be angry when I put myself in that role," she says. "It's not you against me or whether it's right or wrong. My response comes from a place of, 'What message have I been sending that tells someone that it's okay to approach me like that?'"

The CEO of Hattie Hill Enterprises, Inc. has spoken around the globe about human relations in corporate America. Her opinion is sought regularly by *The Wall Street Journal*, *USA Today*, and her hometown newspaper, *The Dallas Morning News*. Clearly, this forty-nine-year-old, awarding-winning entrepreneur is a master communicator and a master connector.

Therefore, when she recently experienced an evening that broke many of the rules of the relationship game, she quickly overcame her shock and responded with her trademark stealth and diplomacy. She practices what the Bible preaches: "The wise weigh their words on a scale with gold."

Before I share her story, let me first explain that everyone who knows Hattie has been well aware that she has been struggling to overcome a life-threatening illness that she contracted from eating bad beef on a cruise ship. For a year, she worked only part-time at her international business consulting company, and she scaled back her professional commitments so that her body could recover.

So you can imagine her shock when—three days after she was released from the Mayo Clinic—a colleague who was well aware of her health crisis invited her to dinner at a nice restaurant and, before dinner was served, asked Hattie to commit to a heavy-duty position on a corporate board—and donate and fundraise $125,000!

Clearly, Hattie's colleague had horrible timing. She was so focused on achieving her own goals, she did not stop to consider whether her proposal was appropriate for Hattie's circumstances at the time.

A key element for a successful "click" in business and in life is to be cognizant of another person's timing. Because when the timing is inappropriate, our first impulse is often to make war with words. And that's the worst way to build and maintain relationships. As the writer Eric Idle once said, "Sticks and stones may break my bones, but words will make me go in a corner and cry by myself for hours."

Still, despite the terrible consequences of verbal attacks, too many folks have not mastered the art of verbal diplomacy. Especially when they encounter unexpected situations like Hattie's dinnertime dilemma. Given those circumstances, too many men and women might explode with an angry, "How *dare* you . . ." or "That is the most inconsiderate, obnoxious proposal. . . ."

So how did Hattie exercise restraint over her response and handle the situation graciously? How did she maintain peace with her words? "I always think before I talk," she says. "I let my friend present her entire case. I didn't just shut her down, I asked more probing questions. Under my 'think before you talk rule,' I ask, 'How do you see this benefiting you?' When I'm going to turn somebody down, I need to know what the win and loss for them is."

Then, when the woman completed her pitch, Hattie calmly responded by saying, "It's not a good time for me. This is where my life is now. You need to find someone who has the time." Hattie also silently resolved to immediately evict this woman from her inner circle. The woman's terrible timing cost her the relationship altogether.

"If someone truly cares about you," Hattie says, "they would stop to think about you first. If she had been pampering my relationship, she would have been saying, 'How are you? Can I bring you food? Can I come to your office and help out?' "

Hattie says she was flabbergasted over the inconsiderate request made by a woman whom Hattie had considered a close friend and respected colleague. But her mouth did not allow her anger, disappointment, and shock to register. Instead, she simply repeated, "I'm not the best person to help you with that at this time."

Hattie says her lack of attention to the insulting request is her way of showing disapproval, because silence speaks loudly. And that complete disregard for the question prompted Hattie's dinner partner to steer the dialogue back to her request.

"She looked at me and said, 'You're not going to do it, are you?' And I said, 'No, but it's okay, sweetie.' And I moved on to a whole other conversation." Meanwhile, Hattie, who wrote the book, *Smart Women, Smart Choices*, felt no need to lambaste the woman with criticism or harsh language. "You can't change other people," she says. "All you can do is change yourself and how you respond to other people."

Hattie feels certain that her communication style works better than the types of verbal assaults that, for too many people, prove irresistible and uncontrollable in similar situations. Instead, she uses scenarios like this to evaluate herself rather than the offender. "I have to question what I am doing that would make another person feel it's okay to say or do a certain thing to me. I may be equally to blame for taking on too many commitments."

Now, she is committed to saying "No" so that she does not over-tax herself. That means, whenever she receives a request, whether considerate or not, she follows one of my favorite rules for communication: think before you talk.

Think Before You Talk

Words have many meanings, depending on who's speaking them and who's hearing them. While you may be tempted to blurt out the first thought that comes to your mind in many situations ("I can't believe you just said that to me" or "That was the most wicked comment I've ever heard" or "Who do you think you are, acting like that?"), it's important to just bite down on the first words that pop into your head when someone makes you angry. Then, when you do speak, use the "mirror technique." In other words, repeat back to the person the exact words he or she said to you.

For example, say your supervisor (we'll call him John) comes into your office at 4:30 on Friday afternoon and says, "We need this project by Monday morning at eight for the board meeting." Your first reaction might to be to lash back with "I can't" or "That's impossible" or "Lack of planning on your part does not create a weekend emergency for me." Others may have a string of exple-tives that are always loaded on the tips of their tongues, ready to fire right back at John or anyone else who pulls their emotional trigger.

As the French philospher Jean-Paul Sartre said, "Words are loaded pistols." But gunfire can be fatal—to relationships and to one's career. So rather than fire off hurtful verbage, you need to cool down. Clearly, tongue-lashing your boss is a surefire way to get stuck on the ladder of success—or shoved off entirely.

So, pause. Repeat John's words back at him. This forces you to resist an emotional response and instead enables you to concentrate on exactly what he said. It keeps you focused on the issue at hand. You're not talking about how angry or frustrated you feel. And you're not venting about how this person gets on your last nerve because he's always overloading you with work that was due an hour ago.

You repeat back, "So what you're saying to me is that you want this project complete by Monday's meeting at eight." You respond, but you don't react. This is good, because when we react, we get sidetracked by the blame game. As a result, all the baggage of this relationship and this work environment gets dumped onto this unrelated situation. The result? A mess. When you focus on the words at hand, however, it gives you time to think of a cool, calm response. It lets you figure out if and how you can get the work done on time.

Now, what if you're the one assigning the project, and your employee makes a costly, embarrassing mistake? How do you confront the person in a way that makes him or her understand the gravity of the error—and teaches the person not to make the same mistake again?

Ask the Offender How He'd Handle the Situation if He Were in Your Shoes

The trick is to get the offender to confess and figure out the solution by himself. Once, when an associate made a blunder that was costly and embarrassing for me and my organization, I was livid. But rather than pepper him with criticism, I handed him the paddle to do it himself. I had him sit in the chair behind my desk. Then I sat facing him, as if he were the boss and I were the employee.

"Okay, Rick," I said, "what would you say if you were me?" Not only did Rick detail how and why the mistake was made, but he outlined a plan to prevent it from happening again. And he's been on his toes ever since!

As the British writer Aldous Huxley said, "Words are tools which automatically carve concepts out of experiences." In my interaction with Rick, we used constructive words to create a new work experience that taught both of us a new, productive way to turn a negative situation into a positive method of improving the way we do business.

While this requires emotional discipline, the rewards are immense. This process forces people to learn a technique that successful people live by: look at a situation from the other person's point of view. It's called empathy. So rather than wonder why I was so mad, Rick could see exactly why I felt the way I did about his error. And Rick was also able to understand how I look at situations at my company. That made him want to work harder and better to keep things efficient, harmonious, and prosperous.

It's also a good lesson on seeing how it feels when things go wrong and we're tempted to use foul language. So:

◆ **Watch your words!** This means putting the "safety" on the assault rifles that our mouths become when firing a barrage of brutal insults. As Eleanor Roosevelt said, "Anger is only one letter short of danger."

So avoid language that creates a negative, combative atmosphere, like "This is war" or "Our sales force is going to battle." Instead, encourage collaboration with clear, positive language: "Each of you has the power to make this company more spectacular tomorrow than it is today."

An excellent way to stay positive is to transform the rage into something more productive, such as writing out "Ten Tactics to Prevent Problems." As you put these ideas into practice, consider the following tactics for making peace, not war, with words when anger suddenly sets off land mines in your relationships. Here are some tactics that may work for you:

◆ **Plan for it.** Upsetting conversations and incidents are going to happen in both your personal and professional interactions. So just as your company holds fire drills with preestablished evacuation plans, you should sketch out a response plan for when disaster strikes with projects, relationships, and deadlines. Your goal is to escape the sparks without fanning the flames with furious words.

To formulate your plan, think about an upsetting situation that tempted you to fire on the offender with scorching words. How did you handle it? Did you explode and cause irreparable harm to the relationship? Did you resort to personal attacks?

Now think about the ideal way for you to respond to an infuriating conversation or scenario. Envision yourself staying cool, as if the offending words roll off a Teflon coating around you. See and hear yourself speaking in a neutral, diplomatic manner. You can even script the exact words that you would say.

For example, if you have a colleague who barks orders in a way that irritates you, perhaps you could prepare to say something like, "Helen, I'd be happy to do that if you'd ask with a please and thank you." While it may feel difficult at first, my experience with speaking up usually results in two things. First, the person becomes aware of their abrasive communication style. And second, they are eager to make up for the past damage they fear they've done, by being extra courteous now and in the future.

Of course, some people enjoy the infliction of verbal abuse. Recognize this and refuse to respond. You can achieve this by thinking a situation through before it happens. Let your mind drift back to a time when that person peppered you with stinging words. Now envision yourself immune and unaffected.

♦ **Step away from the situation.** Sometimes the best way to escape a confrontation is to excuse yourself, go into another room, or tell the person you'll phone them back. Do whatever is necessary to escape the conflict. A change of scene will distract you and enable you to resist the urge to launch a barrage of obscenities at the offender. Remember, when you throw dirt, you lose ground.

♦ **Cool down.** Figure out the best way to vent in the heat of anger. Will taking a walk help you blow off steam? If you're in an office building, climbing a few flights of stairs is a good release; getting the heart pumping will release feel-good endorphins that dissipate anger.

Remember, when you throw dirt, you lose ground.

If you can, hit the gym—and a punching bag. Retreat to your car; let out a primal scream. Go running so your feet can pound your anger into the pavement. Punch your pillow. Take a swim. Write in a journal. Go to the driving range and whack golf balls. Slip away to church, a chapel, a mosque, a synagogue, or other house of worship; the serenity and holiness of the building will instantly calm you. Phone a friend or relative whose voice has a calming effect on you.

The secret to cooling down in the heat of anger depends upon you knowing yourself—and what techniques work best for you.

♦ **Think of the big picture.** If you use your tongue to rip someone to shreds today, where will that leave you tomorrow? Next month? Next year? Will you be destroying a relationship that is important to your work or your personal life? Is it really worth it to indulge a verbal tantrum and risk long-term loss of friendship, income, or reputation?

If you have a hot temper that makes it difficult to stem the flow of criticism once you're upset, consider taking an anger management class or speaking with a counselor to learn techniques for resisting the urge to criticize and potentially crush another person with cruel words.

- **Pinpoint your own problem.** Take a hard look at why certain comments or situations push you into the angry zone. Is your rage motivated by personal peeves or a power trip? Are you being controlling and territorial about how a project is planned and completed? Do you feel cheated or tricked? Is the offender dredging up the pain or humiliation of past problems? Are you projecting onto a situation your own "issues" that are best kept quiet and under control? Self-knowledge is the key to successful anger management. Once you know what makes you tick and why, it will be easier to control your anger when it occurs. So really work to sort through your feelings and identify the root cause of how you respond to negativity; this will help you maintain diplomacy when you speak.

- **Write it out.** Let your anger blast out—on your computer screen or with a pen and paper. But don't push send! And do not mail the letter! Instead, push the delete button or toss the letter in the trash. This way, you discharge the malicious words and feelings—without hurting anyone.

  Writing is a wonderful, safe way to "vent" your emotional response in a way that never jeopardizes your relationships, because the words written in a furious frenzy are never spoken or shared. Since you can never take back spoken words—and verbal attacks can fester in a person's mind for a lifetime—solicit every ounce of discipline to refrain from spewing them. The same goes for a nasty letter—your vitriol can survive for centuries!

As Swedish novelist Frederika Bremer wrote: "There are words which sever hearts more than sharp swords; there are words the point of which sting the heart through the course of a whole life."

So use your pen to help and heal, so that you can create positive solutions for any problem that arises. Another benefit to writing: it slows you down, forcing you to think about how you're feeling and how you will respond to the situation.

If you decide that you should confront the offender, put that in writing as well—by composing a script for the conversation. That way, you have predetermined what you will say and how you will say it.

Start by asking, "How can I use this situation to teach Annie from her mistake?" Then write the script for how you will approach her. Instead of writing, "Annie, you idiot! You really screwed things up!" try: "Annie, I'm really disappointed by how you handled this . . . Knowing your past attention to detail and excellent work, I know you could have done an excellent job. Can you please tell me, what happened?"

By crafting the conversation in writing, you will be able to read back the words and ensure that they sound helpful, not hurtful. This technique endows you with the power of Hollywood moviemaking magic. You set the stage, you create the dialogue, and you bring to life a scene that plays out exactly as you wish.

♦ **When in doubt, don't!** If you're thinking about scolding someone, and you have a gut feeling that maybe it's not their fault, or a confrontation would prove catastrophic to the relationship or situation, then simply zip it. Don't let the words shoot past your lips. Clench your teeth, bite your tongue, cough. Just don't say it!

♦ **Choose your timing wisely.** Orchestrate your confrontation with ideal timing in the best location. Since privacy is imperative, choose an office or conference room; close the door and the window blinds. While some bustling public locations may seem private, you never know who's sitting at the next table in the coffee shop or who's watching from across the restaurant.

As for timing, the middle of the day or the middle of the week is an ideal time to schedule such a heavy-duty conversation. Dropping a verbal bomb on someone at 8:30 A.M. could jeopardize his or her productivity for the day. Likewise, a slew of criticism on a Friday afternoon could cast a cloud over the person's entire weekend.

I find it best to strategize the timing for conversations offering constructive criticism in a way that enables the offender to make amends with a positive performance on a new project. I also give that person the opportunity to use my criticism to correct whatever errors were made. That fills us both with a sense of satisfaction. And it bolsters our relationship by proving that each of us is committed to investing the time, energy, and effort into transforming negatives into positives.

♦ **Communicate face-to-face.** It's cold and impersonal—and it shows indifference—if you convey important information via telephone, e-mail, or fax. Plus, your physical presence conveys a thousand unspoken messages through your tone of voice, facial expressions, and body language. While your words may contain criticisms, the leaning forward position of your body and your gentle tone tell the person, "Listen, I really care about you and your performance. I'm saying this to help you." That nonverbal affirmation will encourage the person to do better.

◆ **Remember that less is more.** To deliver the most memorable message, you should rehearse your lines just as an actor would before taking stage. Several carefully chosen, powerful words will inspire and instruct far more effectively than a long, rambling monologue that leaves your listener glazed over and tuned out.

Perhaps the former vice president Dan Quayle said it best: "Verbosity leads to unclear, inarticulate things." Be clear, be succinct, and you will be understood and remembered.

◆ **Use a soft approach.** Sometimes it's best to mask your criticism under the guise of offering help. If Jodi made a disaster of the monthly report, you could say, "Jodi, I've got some tricks to make your life so much easier! Listen to how I saved tons of time and energy last year when I was in charge of the monthly reports." You can also make it sound like you're lending a helping hand: "Marcus, great news! I'm going to lighten your load by letting Andrew do the proofreading on the memos. That way you're free to handle the website updates without having to worry about anything else."

◆ **Get it done.** If you tell someone you'll write a job recommendation letter, do it. If you promise your niece that you'll speak at her school's Career Day, schedule it in your calendar and show up. And if you vow to complete a project by Friday the 30th, meet the deadline.

Failure to follow through on your own words casts a cloud of distrust, disappointment, and disbelief over your reputation. To paraphrase Ralph Waldo Emerson: *What you do speaks so loudly I can't hear what you say.* In other words, your actions speak louder than words.

I also love what the Norwegian dramatist Henrik Ibsen said: "A thousand words will not leave so deep an impression as one deed." Never underestimate the power of your words—or your actions.

Let each bolster the power of the other. Together they are the building blocks for success in everything we do. In fact, every day I see proof among CEOs, entrepreneurs, and all kinds of folks that the biggest secret to success in business and in life is one's ability to express oneself quickly, easily, and clearly with written and spoken words—and then to practice what you preach.

Job recruiters will tell you that the single most impressive factor among applicants is the ability to articulate one's thoughts into coherent sentences. If people have the added gift of eloquence, that automatically boosts them up the career ladder. The truth is, we crave the sound of well-spoken words. We admire a person who can share ideas with wit, creativity, and diplomacy.

"A thousand words will not leave so deep an impression as one deed."

—Henrik Ibsen

You can become that person, if you put this Truth #8 to work in your life. Remember, as American psychologist Edward Thorndike said, "Colors fade, temples crumble, empires fall, but wise words endure."

Be wise with your words. Time them precisely. And success will be yours.

Exercise for Truth #8

The best way to incorporate this truth into your life is to first understand your own speaking style. So start by evaluating yourself by asking: Do I blurt out the first words that come to mind? Do I say whatever I want, never thinking of the consequences of my words until the damage is done? How has my aggressive speaking style hurt business and relationships? Do I speak diplomatically? Do I carefully choose my words to express myself cautiously yet effectively? Am I an emotional speaker, losing control of my words when I'm angry, sad, or frustrated?

Now, think of three situations in which you lost control of your mouth and spoke hurtful words for the sake of being honest. Take yourself back to the heat of the moment, and then figure out how you could have made peace, not war, with your words. Here are some tips:

> *"Colors fade, temples crumble, empires fall, but wise words endure."*
>
> —American psychologist Edward Thorndike

1. Literally bite your tongue.

2. Walk away.

3. Write it out until you find a diplomatic way to express yourself.

4. Repeat back to the person what they're saying.

5. Take a deep breath and think of the consequences of your words; envision yourself speaking positive words to create a positive outcome.

6. Say, "I need some time to think before I can respond."

You may come up with a more effective method; brainstorm and practice with a friend so that the next time a testy situation arises, you'll make peace, not war, with your words.

Key **CLICK** Factors

Always

♦ Listen actively. If you don't understand what a person means by what they say, either ask or restate your interpretation.

♦ Speak from the heart, find encouraging words, and administer constructive criticism.

Keep in Mind

♦ Silence is golden, and sometimes saying nothing is better than the wrong words at the wrong time.

♦ When bonding or reconciling, personal notes are more effective than cards, cards are more effective than e-mails, and e-mails are more effective than nothing.

Do Not

♦ Speak before you think.

♦ Say the first thing that comes to mind if you are upset.

♦ Get personal. Keep the constructive criticism upbeat and nurturing.

Make Sure To

♦ Frame your words to suit your audience if you want to have productive conversation.

♦ Use empathetic and compassionate words in times of hardship and crisis. The right words at the right time can be life changing.

Be Open to Everything and Attached to Nothing; the Best Idea Wins

---

As you think, so shall you be. So flush out all old, tired, worn-out thoughts. Fill your mind with fresh, new creative thoughts of faith, love and goodness. By this process you can actually remake your life.

—Norman Vincent Peale in *The Power of Positive Thinking*

YOUR MIND IS like a colorful parachute; it is beautiful and powerful when it's open! You witness its magnificent strength and brilliance only when the parachute expands with air and reflects light. The same goes for your brain; when people could not see the light, the truth, that era was called the Dark Ages. Now, when we choose new relationships and stay open to attracting like-minded colleagues, we explore new, vast horizons of life's riches. This can help you triumph over the one constant in life: change.

Your mind is like a colorful parachute; it is beautiful and powerful when it's open!

Orrin C. Hudson has the power to transform almost any child—delinquent, depressed, or just disinterested in learning—into a chess champion. And through the mastery of the game, Hudson is rerouting thousands of boys and girls from a life predicted by inner-city statistics to new, exciting adventures in accomplishment and success.

"Everyone can be someone if they simply make the right move," says Orrin, a former Alabama state trooper who saw too many people dying or going to jail for making the wrong moves. In fact, when he heard about five people getting killed in a robbery for $2,400, he left his job at a successful car dealership to found a nonprofit organization that helps boys and girls escape a plethora of dead-end and even deadly choices.

Since 2001, Be Someone, Inc. has taught seventeen thousand children how to triumph at chess and in life. Orrin does this through his visionary style of connecting with children to transform their potential tragedies into winning strategies.

In fact, his efforts to instill character, hope, and inspiration within disadvantaged youth have been featured on CNN, NBC News, Court TV, and the Angel Network. Superstars like Jane Fonda, along with the motivational speakers Les Brown and Tony Robbins, have praised his efforts, and so do I. In fact, Orrin received the 2007 FraserNet Community Service Award at my annual PowerNetworking Conference. His musical performance and speech inspired a standing ovation and cash donations to his organization.

Similarly, Orrin's infectious energy mesmerized me when I met him four years ago. As he introduced me as a speaker at a Success Tour in his hometown of Atlanta, he roused the audience by saying, "There's a new currency on the planet. KASH. Knowledge, Attitude, Skills, and Habits. No one can take it away from you, and it makes you rich beyond compare."

As Orrin spoke, we clicked. Because his message echoed my way of thinking. And the timing was right. At that phase of my life, something about Orrin's message struck a powerful chord in my mind and heart. Had I heard him twenty years prior to that day, perhaps his message would not have clicked with me. But the timing was right for me to "get" what he was saying, and a fruitful relationship has flourished between us ever since.

Though we had just met, I knew that we shared a life purpose and passion for helping people; that connects us. And so, in just a few minutes, he showed that we can immediately click with another person when our intuition responds positively to how they act, what they say, and what energy they exude. Of course, we can also disconnect, when we meet someone whose words, actions, or demeanor insults, offends, or gives off a bad vibe.

> "Everyone can be someone if they simply make the right move."
>
> —Orrin C. Hudson, founder of Be Someone, Inc.

But in Orrin's case, I was feeling his positive message to help people. As he regaled the crowd with tales of how he can play chess blindfolded—as anyone can, if they try—his enthusiasm and upbeat words radiated liked sunshine around him. Then and now, he infuses everyone with an unstoppable, can-do spirit. That's why the two-time Atlanta chess champion travels the country to train at-risk children to become victors in the game of chess and the game of life.

I asked Orrin to share a story about one child whose life he transformed by encouraging the youngster to keep an open mind about the seemingly mysterious, intellectual game of chess. Orrin chuckles as he remembers one special boy. "His mom had nicknamed him 'The Child from Hell.' Raynard (not his real name) was fourteen years old and doing drugs, carrying guns, doing everything bad. When I met him, he had just gotten expelled from school for carrying a loaded gun to class!"

Orrin met the teen at a Georgia boot camp, where he was invited to do chess training for fifty students. "This was a place where it's your last chance before you go to jail," Orrin says. "Raynard became one of my star students. He gravitated to the top by paying attention and being in the moment."

But in order for Orrin to connect with children like Raynard—who seem lost in the distraction of crime, music, videos, fashion, and rebellion—the forty-five-year-old must first take himself back to when he was a fourteen-year-old delinquent on the streets of Birmingham, Alabama.

As one of thirteen children growing up in a rough housing project, he says, "I was so poor, I was wearing my brothers' hand-me-down pants. Those jeans were worn so thin, I could sit on a dime and tell you if it was heads or tails."

So to make money, Orrin launched an illegal enterprise. "At the time, my hustle was stealing inner-tubes and selling them for a quarter each," says Orrin. "Until I walked into my all-black high school and a white teacher walked up to me and said, 'Orrin, every action you take has consequences. Let me teach you chess.'"

At first, Orrin questioned why he'd want to spend time playing the seemingly boring board game that he viewed as a traditionally white and very complicated pursuit. But Orrin said even in the midst of his bad-boy mind-set, something deep inside urged him to have an open mind and try something new and better than what he was doing. So what finally convinced him to try it? A heartfelt connection with the teacher.

"That teacher cared about me," Orrin said. "I could tell that he was genuine. He bought me a chess book, the only book I ever had. No one ever told me to read but him! Isn't that crazy?! The teacher said, 'All readers are leaders. To earn more, you've got to learn more. (Orrin now has 800 books in his house!) And no one's coming to the rescue. You've got to pull your own self up. You cannot hire someone else to do your push-ups. The magic formula is to do the work yourself.' " And that work, when it comes to strategizing victory, Orrin says, is all about patterns—on the chessboard and in real life.

"The teacher taught me pattern recognition," Orrin says. "If you successfully follow the clues, if you make the right moves on the chessboard, you'll win. Always. The chessboard doesn't care; it's neutral. Nature is the same way. Life plays no favorites. If you play the right way in life, you win. Period."

Those words stayed with Orrin as he boosted his grades "from dumb to the honor roll. Nobody can tell you you're stupid if you beat them at chess." By competing with college students at a local campus, Orrin mastered the art of capturing his opponent's king with such finesse that he once beat a Russian international master in eighteen moves. Victory turbocharged his self-esteem; this is the essence of what he instills in children.

With rap-style rhythm and repetition, Orrin walks the classroom chanting, "Stay in the moment, stay in the moment, say it! Stay in the moment!" By focusing on the task at hand, he says children can block out all the negative distractions and learn concentration skills. And the game of chess teaches them that with every move, you either win or you learn. That's what Orrin said as he walked the classroom at the Georgia boot camp, repeating, "One, two, turn! Help me out, class! One, two, turn! You can do it, class! One, two, turn!" The pieces on the board are like people, he tells them, and when you strategize with the right ones, you win. Easily.

So how did Orrin click with Raynard? "Raynard was receptive when he saw that I'm genuine," Orrin says. "Sometimes a child needs to borrow your faith until their faith kicks in. You have to make them think they're someone. I always say to a class, 'Everyone in here can be president of the United States, when you believe.' "

Trying new ideas breaks us away from old, self-defeating patterns that block success, Orrin says. "Most people are afraid to get in the game because they're afraid they'll lose. You've got to recognize that you've got to be willing to make mistakes because we learn more from losing than from winning. And that makes it okay." So he asks his students to chant along with him: "Get in the game! Get in the game! Say it! Get in the game!"

Showing love to everyone makes it easy for Orrin to encourage curiosity in something new, without being preachy or aggressive. "I was a state trooper for six years. I had the blue light, the badge, and the gun. But I treated everyone I met like they were the most important person in the world. I'm a nice guy; I uplift and inspire everyone I meet, everywhere I go, so I try to get people to get in the game. Say it! Get in the game!"

This high-energy style enables Orrin to make learning so much fun that he coached elementary students to beat high school students at chess, taking a last place team to three straight championships.

Orrin says when he teaches children and adults how to master this seemingly complex game, he's simply showing them how to tap into the talent and ability that's hiding under fear and low self-esteem. When they start winning and applying the ideas to life, he likes to think of himself as the lightbulb that's illuminating the brains and ability that they already have.

"I'm an optometrist," he says playfully. "I help people see what's already there. If you go in a dark room, you can't see anything. If I turn the light on, you see the sofa, the refrigerator, the chairs. So I show people what was already there. A magic formula! I go around turning on lights. I show that you can do some incredible things with your life, if you're willing to learn from everyone you meet."

His mother recently proved that once again. "My mom called me and said, 'Orrin, this drunk in the neighborhood came by the house and told me that I am watering poison oak.' She told him to get lost. I said, 'Mom, listen to him and check it out.' And she called me back a week later; she said the professional garden people said poison oak had deflowered her new plant and she was, in fact, watering poison oak, just like the drunk told her. Everyone you meet is your what? Teacher!"

And with a new mind-set comes a new language, Orrin says, for adults and children. "I write 'try' and 'can't' on the board, then erase them and say, 'Erase these out of your mind. Don't ever use them because you never know what you can do until you take action. The key to success is taking action.' "

And that's what happened with Raynard. Orrin says he worked with the boy, teaching him chess strategies, and he won a championship. "Now Raynard is a productive citizen and he's living his dream, working at the airport," Orrin says. "The key thing that made his life successful was that I made him realize that no one's coming to the rescue. For your life to get better, you have to get better. Not the government, not the president, and not anybody but you!"

Clicking with young people has earned Orrin the NAACP Community Service Award, the National Self-Esteem Award, the

Black Enterprise Magazine Everyday Hero Award, the TBS Super-station Pathfinder for Education Award, the MLK Award, and the Harvard Black Law Student Community Service Award.

The U.S. Air Force veteran says his spirit arrives just in time to save young lives from tragedy. "Three years ago, I showed up at a school in Kentucky, and a kid said he was going to kill himself," Orrin says, "and when he heard my message, he told me he wasn't going to. At another school, a boy came to me crying. He said, 'You're the only black teacher I've ever seen in this school.' I could see in his eyes that he was amazed and inspired. Things like that let me know I'm doing what God made as my calling."

And it all started at age fourteen with an open mind—Orrin's rule number one. "If you said to me, 'Hey, Orrin, you've been spelling your name wrong for forty years,' I'm willing to spell my name differently because I'm open and learning."

Now, just like Abraham Lincoln's mother told him to "Be some-one," Orrin says he's keeping that spirit alive by empowering young people to do all they can do. "If you're going to be a street sweeper, be the best one anyone's ever seen. Just make the right move and get in the game!"

Orrin Hudson is uplifting and inspiring children every day because he's using the most powerful machine on the planet. Everyone has one. You know, that small gray object that weighs about three pounds. The human brain.

"The universe is a very rich place if you just leave yourself open."

—actor Richard Gere

It's smarter than a computer; it created computers! "Man is still the most extraordinary computer of all," John F. Kennedy said. But time, circumstance, and negative thinking have locked many people's minds into air-tight tombs that repel new ideas and innovation. And that, in our super-speed world, is a surefire formula for failure.

"Life brings so much, and it's better when you're not looking for it," says actor Richard Gere, a devout Buddhist. "The universe is a very rich place if you just leave yourself open. So much comes."

But most people try to force things to happen, even though the most magical connections happen naturally. So how can you open your mind to new, powerful ideas that could transform the way you live, love, and do business?

Replace Judgment with Patience and Curiosity

Always remember Romans 2:1: "Quench the urge to judge." Even when you think you've got the inside scoop on a situation, remember that things are rarely as they appear. There's always much more going on than the surface implies, and the best way to get answers is to ask.

When you get answers, listen and act with your heart. Your heart is your interpersonal radar device; it will pound loudly when you connect with a special person or idea. Too many of us, though, let our old, inefficient ways of doing things shut out this inner voice of wisdom. We let past baggage block intuition, and we lose out. We have to let our hearts guide us in business and in life by listening to that inner voice and acting on what we hear. How? By listening with a deep desire to learn. Every person we meet is a virtual encyclopedia of life lessons and experiences that can make us wiser. But we're not hearing that. We need to relearn the art of really absorbing what people are saying. Remember, with every experience we have in life, one of two things happens: either we win or we learn. We never lose.

We either make a great connection that endures for a reason, a season, or a lifetime, or we learn a lesson from that person and move on. Too often these days, listening has degenerated into being quiet while you wait for your turn to talk. True listening is about clearing your thoughts and letting the other person's words, ideas, and emotions register on your open mind. Why? Because we're listening for those magic words that make us click. All the while, I'm going through my mental inventory to find things that might connect to what this person is saying. I am searching for common ground. And heart.

This requires slowing down, staying in the moment, forcing our brains to stop multitasking or ticking down a to-do list while we nod vacantly at the speaker. Really listen and analyze, and see if what the person is saying can produce mutually powerful, profitable ideas and plans. The only way I can win is if you win.

When I'm at a book signing or a speech, my passion for people and my lifelong desire to learn inspire the way I interact with complete strangers: with warmth and love. I view every human being with whom I come into contact as a living, breathing life lesson for me. Each is a mystery, a puzzle. And all I have to do is smile, say a few leading words, and voilà: this new person opens up and shares new knowledge that enriches my life. And in some odd way, we are connecting. All the while, my interest in them fosters a sense of belonging for them.

The only way I can win is if you win.

The trick is to pay attention and get the other person talking. If a woman has impeccably manicured hands, a simple, "Your nails are stunning" will have her smiling all day. She feels appreciated, celebrated, and that exchange sparks positive energy that only gains momentum throughout both your days. It may sound simple or even shallow. But she didn't pay fifty bucks to get her nails done if she didn't want someone to notice. That's what makes her feel good. So indulge her, and yourself; her smile will light up your day. And her conversation may teach you something.

While you're taking in all this new information, back up opinions and recommendations with facts. Just:

◆ **Plug into the electronic age!** The Internet can be your high-speed pass to success. If you think you can excel in today's world without the instant communication and information that the Internet puts at your fingertips—you're wrong. The World Wide Web saves you time, energy, and money. It is your one-stop success source regarding your health, your wealth, and your professional endeavors. So if you've been adamantly refusing to hop onto the information superhighway, please reconsider. Ask a friend or colleague for a tutorial or take a class on how to navigate the vastness of cyberspace.

◆ **Change your outlook about work and your work will change—for the better!** I guarantee—if you start to think of your job as fun, even entertaining, then you'll enjoy yourself so much that you'll forget it's work. Likewise, if you view your job as torturous drudgery, it will feel that way. This same idea applies to relationships. If you recast your thoughts about your neighbor, for example, from "that grumpy guy who always complains about the weather" to "the grill master who sizzles up the greatest steaks around" then you'll feel more positive about him.

This boils down to thinking positive and embracing the change that life always brings. The problem? Most people loathe change. Rather than end a bad relationship, they'd rather have the "company" than be alone. Instead of quitting a miserable job, they'd rather keep complaining and maintain the security of the paycheck. Plus, it's easier to sit on the couch drinking a beer and watching television than to do the hard work of soul-searching and finding out how you truly can serve others in a positive way and enjoy yourself while doing it.

◆ **Unleash the power of your mind.** Believe what Jonas Ridderstråle and Kjell Nordström, who wrote the book *Funky Business*, had to say in an article by Jim Pawlack in the *Cleveland*

Plain Dealer: "We own the major assets of society—our own minds. And power equals freedom. We are all potentially free to know, go, do and be whoever we want to be." This type of thinking advocates the idea that our minds hold the answers to immense creativity that can launch us on our way to achieving great personal and professional accomplishments. Brainstorm, then begin to put your innovative ideas to work!

◆ **Write down your flashes of brilliance.** Ideas are electricity firing the synapses in our brains. Your thoughts and ideas are blasting through your brain at lightning-fast speed, which means they're here one split-second, gone the next. If you don't write them down, poof—priceless, original ideas are gone. Keep something—a small notepad, a PDA, a laptop—handy at all times; some artists actually write on their own skin when they think of song lyrics! One writer I know carries paper and pen while jogging because that's when her best ideas snap! crackle! and pop! in her brain. Whatever works!

Fully Explore a Person, Proposal, or Criticism Before Responding or Making a Decision

How many times have you uttered, "No" or "That's impossible" or "We can't" before someone has even finished talking? Some dusty trapdoor in the recesses of your mind slams shut over the new idea, while your old way of thinking shouts, "We've never done it that way!" And you respond just as quickly.

But a closed mind cheats you of an opportunity. So practice saying, "That's innovative. Let me think about it." Or: "That's a radical change but I'm open to how it might work for me."

First, find out as much as you can about the idea from the Internet and from talking to other people. See if this hot new idea is all the rage. I remember an encyclopedia salesman told me in the 1980s that one day the big heavy books would be obsolete because information would be stored on a small silver circle called a compact disc. It seemed hard to believe then, but now CDs and DVDs are a part of our daily life and it's the multivolume encyclopedia that seems odd!

Be Willing to Change the Way You Work and Play

Diversify! In today's global economy, it's crucial to cultivate relationships with people from a spectrum of races, religions, countries, and cultures. Being savvy about cultural differences will make you more sensitive and appealing.

Nervous about being politically correct? Start by taking a diversity workshop and learn from the experts how to become more inclusive in business and in life. You cannot single-handedly solve racism and bigotry in America, but you can solve it in your own life.

And the way we do that is through close, personal friendships. When you're breaking bread and engaging someone who does not look like you, you're melting away the barriers and biases that divide us. When you model that for children, you're eradicating racism from the next generation.

I have gay and lesbian friends, and knowing them has completely changed the way I view the gay community from the way I did twenty-five years ago. They are people who love, live, and laugh just like I do, and when we relate as human beings I don't think of them as gay, but rather as my friends who love spy novels, butter pecan ice cream, and playing the stock market.

Another tip: Design your way to success. Design is so critical that it should be on every businessperson's agenda to "brand" their products, services, meetings, and conferences. That means putting your unique logo and style on everything you do so that it is as instantly recognizable as the Nike swoosh or the Mercedes-Benz symbol.

If you haven't invested in design because you thought it was an extravagance, think again. It's an investment in your success. Think about it: every time your logo is out there, people see it. They become familiar with your brand. And that makes them more comfortable soliciting your services. Next time you're in the store buying cola, do you reach for the generic brand or do you choose Coke or Pepsi? Chances are, you grab one of the most recognizable brands on the planet, because you trust its quality. Brand means trust, and trust means everything in business and in life. I can't stress enough that small businesses that ignore the power of elegant and functional design will lose. Period.

Every night you should ask yourself, "Have I learned something new today?" If not, take a class, go to a meeting, join a club or a church. Don't live a one-track life. Just as you diversify your investment portfolio, diversify your life! Very successful people are connected to seven groups or communities. That's twice as many as the average professional or affluent person. Having so many influences makes you more interesting and satisfied, and better informed on many topics.

As Norman Vincent Peale said in *The Power of Positive Thinking*, an open mind can give you the power of positive living. "The secret of a better and more successful life is to cast out those old, dead, unhealthy thoughts," Peale wrote. I would also add "people" to that list. Substitute for them new, vital, dynamic thoughts and people. You can depend on it—an inflow of new thoughts and people will remake you and your life.

Exercise for Truth #9

We all have preconceived notions about certain things. But they block us from clicking with new, exciting people. So it's time to open our minds and embrace innovative ideas and experiences. You can start by making a list of things that you're stuck on. For example, you may say, "I never pay my bills online. I prefer sending old-fashioned checks in the mail." You can open your mind to the convenience and speed of online bill paying by talking with a friend who does it. Try it once and you may discover that it's trustworthy and time-saving.

Another example: You may boast, "I have never tried sushi. Raw fish is disgusting." Open your mind and your mouth to a new experience by joining an associate for lunch at a sushi restaurant. Order California rolls and other forms of the delicacy that do not include raw fish. Try the ginger and the wasabi—you might become a sushi enthusiast!

Think about habits and attitudes that you've developed over the years that may be holding you back from making money or new friends. Have the courage to face those fears—and enjoy the thrill of new people, places, and things.

Habits Holding You Back	Possible Outcomes if Changed Habits
1.	
2.	
3.	
4.	
5.	

Key **CLICK** Factors

Always
- Be flexible.
- Be at ease with yourself and others.
- Listen actively.

Keep in Mind
- Personal experience is a poor measure on which to base broad and important decision-making.
- Only reliable data collection and analysis from as many perspectives as possible yield reliable information for the best and most effective decisions.

Do Not
- Prejudge; instead, think before you talk, cool off, and respond later.
- Compete; cooperation is the key.
- Be generic. Rather, discover and then articulate your attributes.

Make Sure To
- Always keep an open mind.
- See the strengths, not the limitations, in others.
- Make people proud to be themselves—tell them they are special.

It Takes Teamwork to Make the Dream Work

Coming together is a beginning, staying together is progress, and working together is success.

—Henry Ford

TEAMWORK MAKES THE dream work! And those with the strongest teams triumph on the battlefield of life. Sizing up people is critical, so recruit trustworthy allies who share common ground with your values and vision, your likes and dislikes. But also choose people who are confident enough to challenge you to embrace bigger and better ideas. First, however, make sure your strategy is strong and your self-confidence is indomitable.

Power couple Kym and Sandra Yancey had a dream—to create an online community for women to network and do business with each other. Their pioneering idea attracted top-notch experts who wanted to join their team. For the wrong reasons.

"When I interviewed these people," says Kym Yancey, the fifty-two-year-old cofounder and president of eWomenNetwork.com, "I got the feeling that they were excited about my idea because they thought this would be a great account and that it would generate a big fee for their services."

But that profit-focused mentality did not click with the altruistic vision that Kym and Sandra shared for their dream enterprise. "We are entrepreneurs who focus on service first," Kym says from their headquarters in Dallas, Texas. "Our philosophy is that when you expand the success of someone else, you create success for yourself. So we serve our members."

With that philosophy in mind, back in July 1999 Kym and Sandra embarked on a quest to recruit only like-minded experts to their team. And they used an unconventional approach to money to do that. "I looked for people who loved our dream," Kym says, as he and Sandra sought the best Web development team, the most outstanding graphic designers, excellent attorneys, and superior website technology experts for their team. He says the companies that reviewed their proposal as a cut-and-dry money-making deal would respond by quoting a dollar figure for what their services would cost. That conversation, in the world of commerce and companies, is what you would expect in the normal course of business.

But it was not the way the Yanceys wanted to do it. And anyone who did it that way did not get the deal. Instead, Kym clicked with the perfect members of his dream team when they spoke the magic words—a desire to share in bringing a pioneering dream to life, with the goal of serving others to thrive in business and in life.

"When I found the right people, they said, 'We want to be a part of your vision,' " Kym recalls, "which is what I wanted to hear. They not only loved the idea, but they believed in it to the point that they were willing to put in the labor and time." These were people who naturally clicked with the Yanceys' philosophy, motive, and vision for the company.

The idea of eWomenNetwork was inspired by Sandra's decades of experience in corporate America, where she found that networking with women was icy and ineffective. Too often, she would attend a reception where women clustered in impenetrable cliques.

Feeling frustrated and shut out of opportunities for new business, she brainstormed to conceive a solution with Kym. Together they wondered, "How many other women must be suffering through this networking nightmare? And how can we help them meet other women in ways that spark new business opportunities for them?" Kym and Sandra pooled their decades of experience to conceive their dream.

As the former drummer and lead singer for the band Sun, which had a recording deal with Capitol Records from 1976 to 1981, Kym later created a jingle production company and full-service advertising agency with twenty employees and $20 million in annual revenue. Over the course of fifteen years, Kym says his company won more than 200 advertising and marketing awards. After selling the company in 1996 and moving to Dallas, Kym immersed himself in the world of the Internet as vice president of specialty markets for Matchmaker.com.

Meanwhile, Sandra was thriving in the corporate world as an organization development specialist at LexisNexis. The timing in their lives "clicked"—they both craved change and the freedom of embarking on their own entrepreneurial dream. And so, with Sandra's unpleasant networking experiences and Kym's creative and business expertise—they teamed up to serve women with their innovative solution. And the result is eWomenNetwork.com.

"We wanted to create the ultimate good old girl network," Kym says playfully. In fact, it is a modern twist on that. The eWomen-Network website is where female entrepreneurs pay to join and maintain a Web page that includes a picture, a bio, and a description of their products and services. Visitors have the opportunity to e-mail each member directly and conduct detailed geographic searches to find, for example, an interior designer, a business coach, or an accountant.

In addition, 113 chapters around the United States host monthly events at which women can meet face-to-face to network in a warm, nurturing environment. That feeling manifests at an annual international conference in Dallas, Kym says, that caters to women with awards ceremonies and such touches as fresh rose petals adorning the bathrooms.

When the women come together, Kym says, the spirit of giving and serving is so powerful that forty-two local chapters each donated $750 to purchase a van for a member who operates a safe house and counseling service for abused women who are deaf.

The woman, Julie Rems-Smario, who is deaf, had won the Humanitarian of the Year Award, Kym says, and her interpreter had stood on stage doing the sign for applause: raising her hands over her head.

"It was amazing to see a huge room full of women who went silent and all waved their hands over their heads," Kym recalls. "When you open a conference like that, it sets the tone. The next day everybody was so interested in how they could help each other on a deep spiritual and emotional level."

Kym and Sandra are bringing to life the powerful words of Napoleon Hill, author of *Think and Grow Rich*: "It is literally true that you can succeed best and quickest by helping others to succeed." And so it is no surprise that such a powerful chemistry of goodwill manifests at the eWomenNetwork conference, Kym says, because the company was founded on that very principle as the couple assembled their dream team.

They wanted every member of their team to approach their innovative idea with passion and enthusiasm that equaled their own. "Nothing is as important as having a unified group of people who share in the exact same dream as you have to the point that they're willing to sacrifice and take a bullet with you," Kym adds. "If you go down, they go down."

Their chosen team members' commitment to work, to sacrifice, and to risk their investment in a novel concept proved their allegiance to the team—because they were not being paid up front. Then how were they compensated? "When they came on board," Kym says, "I gave them a percentage of the company to launch what we needed to do."

The only person they paid from the beginning, Kym says, is the person who runs the operations for eWomenNetwork. And to demonstrate her commitment to the vision, she had left a high-paying position to accept a fraction of her salary in order to join the Yanceys' team. "Now she's getting double in salary what she made before joining us," Kym says, "and when you factor in her stock in the company, she's a millionaire."

> *"It is literally true that you can succeed best and quickest by helping others to succeed."*
>
> —author Napoleon Hill

Similarly, the company's chief technology officer—who is responsible for all of the technology that makes the website work— is receiving tremendous profits now after giving freely of his time and talent to launch eWomenNetwork in September 2000.

Kym says that his company is now the biggest revenue source for both the chief technology officer and the graphic artist team that created the cybernetworking community that now includes more than five hundred thousand women in North America.

All of this is proof, Kym says, that "You can build your dream without cash. You can sell your dream with other people and share the wealth." Kym adds that the secret to his success when building their dream team boils down to the fact that deep down, everyone wants to share in something meaningful.

As the writer Denis Waitley said, "No man or woman is an island. To exist just for yourself is meaningless. You can achieve the most satisfaction when you feel related to some greater purpose in life, something greater than yourself."

And when that desire is a more powerful motivation than money—because the reward is an immeasurably wonderful sense of fulfillment—then it's possible to connect with the perfect players for success. In essence, the chemistry, fit, and timing all synchronize to turbocharge a team to score victories for themselves, the team, and the countless people their efforts will help.

> *"You can achieve the most satisfaction when you feel related to some greater purpose in life, something greater than yourself."*
>
> —writer Denis Waitley

"This is the ultimate clicking," Kym says. And removing money from the initial conversation is a powerful litmus test that reveals just how deeply each person endorses the dream. The depth of that endorsement determines whether they win a spot on the team.

But few entrepreneurs understand this lesson when they're building their dream teams, Kym says. "So many people let money be their stopping zone," he says. "I hear it all the time. They say, 'I'm broke. I need people to invest in my company. I need to get a million-dollar loan to make it happen.' "

Kym's response is to inspire them to open their minds to view their dream differently. He does that by asking, "Have you thought of selling your concept to people and giving them a piece of the dream?" In doing so, he says that people are buying into the depth of the relationship with faith that they will ultimately prosper financially as well.

"People buy into relationships," he says. "People buy into facial expressions. People buy into enthusiasm. People buy into passion. People buy into dreams." And once they join the dream team, Kym says, the formula for success is "the three T's: talking, time, and touch."

Talking is the tool for open, honest communication that must be ongoing and comprehensive of every angle and issue involved in starting and succeeding in business and relationships.

The second T is *time*. "You must invest time with people," Kym says, because that provides the opportunity to talk, to build trust, and to get to know each other. It's imperative, he says, to build and maintain strong bonds with everyone on your team—your spouse, your children, your friends, your mentor (Kym says "femtor"), your attorney, your graphic artist, your financial adviser, etc. That time can manifest as a lunch date, a phone call, a chat over coffee, or a day on the golf course.

The third T, Kym says, is *touch*. "It's a nice touch on the back when appropriate," he says, "or touching the heart, touching the soul with words and actions. If any one of these is absent from the formula, the team breaks down. Ask anybody whose marriage is falling apart, and at least one of those is missing."

In his own marriage, Kym says, he and Sandra—who is not only a cofounder but also the CEO of eWomenNetwork—refer to their teamwork in terms of a sandbox. To them, the sandbox symbolizes the specific areas of the business that each one of them officially handles.

"We each have our own sandbox," he says. "If I want to get in her sandbox, I ask permission to get in her sandbox, and I never violate that respect."

For example, Kym says, Sandra handled the decorations for their conference. "I would never dream of going out and buying a great centerpiece for the table at the conference," he says. "Instead, I would say, 'Hey, I saw something you might like' and I show her a picture so she can make the decision." Likewise, Kym says, his wife respects his turf in the company. "I handle sales and marketing," he says. "She doesn't go talk to them about her great new idea. She talks to me."

These smooth operations, however, grew out of bumpy beginnings. Kym explains, "In the beginning I didn't show her the respect she deserves. She would do things and I'd say, 'Here's a better way to do it.' I had to step back and say, 'Hey, she knows what she's doing.' I had to listen more and talk less."

Ultimately, Kym says, the secret for success in building a team to manifest a dream is that it's about helping people. "The formula for success is, 'Come and give,' " he says. "People want to take an 'instant pill' to make their business an overnight success. That's not the way to do it. It's about engaging your team and sharing with them where you're going, and showing them that what they do is significant. That creates success for the members of my team, for me, and for the people we serve with eWomenNetwork."

Write Out Your Goals, Your Plan for Reaching Them, and the List of People You Will Recruit to Help You Climb the Ladder of Success

Kym and Sandra Yancey provide powerful testimony to the importance of careful team building. But you'll notice that before they set out to recruit people, they started with a vision of their business. They wrote out a detailed plan of exactly how they would create eWomenNetwork, how it would operate, and what responsibilities each team member would handle.

By putting their plan in writing, they were following the wisdom of the ancient Egyptian pharaoh Ramses as portrayed in the movie *The Ten Commandments*, when he so eloquently said: "And so it is written, and so it is done."

Once you have your team in place, it's imperative that you adjust, in writing, your goals and ideas in the context of what unique talents each team member brings to the company. Seeing your plans in black and white is the first step toward making them live, Technicolor realities.

Personally, I write out my own goals, whether they're for the hour, the month, the year, or a decade. Once I set expectations for myself, I then focus on what I expect of my team: my office staff, the folks who help coordinate my annual PowerNetworking Conference, and key members of my network who involve me in their innovative programs around the globe. For each of these groups of people, I prepare a concise outline of goals and objectives that we, together, strive to achieve over a specific period of time.

Using teamwork to make the dream work requires continuous effort—hourly, daily, weekly, monthly, yearly. Think about that as you train your team for action. Take comfort in the fact that you are well ahead of the game by simply having a team and goals in the first place. I always say, the most important goal in life is to have a goal at all. We need goals as individuals, as members of a team, and as a unified team. We must all work together to score the points in one unified effort.

And I'm not talking about setting just one goal either; we actually need many goals. But most people do not have *any* goals. They are mired in the mind-numbing mediocrity of a work-a-day life at a job they loathe. They never took the time to map out a plan and set goals; they just let life string them along, day by day, year by year. And if you don't know where you're going, any road will take you there.

So how do you set goals? First, ask what is the number one thing you want to achieve during your lifetime? For me, I want to be remembered—I want to have made a difference.

Then set smaller goals: where you want to be in five years, ten years. What will you have accomplished? How much money will you be earning? Also identify what you want to achieve over the next year, the next quarter, the next month.

Then break it down by days and weeks by asking, "What do I need to do today, this week, to work toward reaching my goals?"

What you do every day counts, even simple things like making a phone call or clipping a news article that teaches you a better way to do business. When you're losing weight, every workout gets you closer to your goal. When you're saving money, every penny adds up. Your efforts and actions toward your life and career goals work the same way. Everything counts.

But first things first, second things never. In other words, focus and do the first thing on your list, then the second thing becomes the first thing and so on. For me, as I work toward lifetime goals, I strategize in quarterly blocks; I set out to accomplish a specific list of goals every three months.

And I get to work. Work is the operative word here, whether you're working alone or with your team. There's no way around it: *You gotta put in the work.* Otherwise your goals and dreams are just words. And there's no such thing as starting at the top. It takes action to make it happen!

So how do you eat this elephant? One bite at a time. Day by day. Because days add up to a lifetime. That's why every evening I write my to-do list for the next day: an hour-by-hour breakdown for meetings, exercise, meals, travel, research, and speaking engagements. This creates my daily plan to micromanage my Big Picture strategy.

As you write the plan that you will instruct your team to implement, sketch out the seemingly smallest details. For example, if you're starting a company, write down every facet of the business that you can think of: products, services, quality control, advertising, expansion, your location and building, the specific roles that each employee will play, insurance, the seasonal rhythm of sales and how to adjust merchandise accordingly (if you sell skis, then clearly you should sell summer sporting goods during the warmer months).

Brainstorm every aspect of the above items with your team. They may consider angles or issues that never crossed your mind. Even if you think you're the expert, don't try to play the all-knowing captain without consulting the experts that you handpicked for the job.

As basketball player Kareem Abdul-Jabbar said, "One man can be a crucial ingredient on a team, but one man cannot make a team."

Constantly remind the team that your business is about serving people. Always ask, "Where can my services do the most good?" For example, if you own a security company, and you know that the local convenience store chain is having a big problem with robberies, brainstorm how you can tailor a security program to meet that company's specific needs. Your service is making customers and

> *"One man can be a crucial ingredient on a team, but one man cannot make a team."*
>
> —Kareem Abdul-Jabbar

employees feel safe as well as saving the company money lost through theft.

Your plan should include a timetable that realistically addresses the time and talent that each team member brings to the business. For example, if your graphic artist says that your website will be complete in two months, then consider that timeframe when you schedule the launch of your e-business.

Also, be cognizant of obstacles that you and your team members may face in their personal or professional lives. Is your graphic designer recovering from a surgery that is slowing her down? Did your attorney recently suffer the death of a spouse and as a result is processing paperwork much more slowly? Has anything been holding you back? Are you nursing an elderly parent? Need more education or training? Recovering from a car accident? Now write out a strategy to manage each obstacle, for yourself and for your team members, so you can proceed.

I had an obstacle for twelve years when I was working at a Fortune 500 company. I had to keep that job to feed my family and provide health benefits. I was not always happy, but I did not want to jeopardize my family's well-being by leaping into a speaking and writing career before I had the respect and name recognition to earn significant income. So during those twelve years, I strategized. I honed my speaking skills. I mapped the course I would take when the time was right. Then, when my children were older, I was prepared to begin my speaking, writing, and traveling. And the world was ready for me.

But first, to climb onward and upward, I had to write out a strategy. And since I could not become a world-class speaker or best-selling author by myself, I had to practice what I preach: Network! I had to assemble a team of people who were on my side, who would—after I served them—help me climb the ladder of success.

I always kept in mind Ecclesiastes 4:9, 10: "Recognize that others increase your worth."

So I invested years of cultivating important relationships to position myself in a spot where I do what I'm doing—speaking, writing, and hosting the nation's most stellar networking conference every June.

It all started with an idea, goals, and a plan and a list of all the people who could help me. Who do you need on your team to bring your dream(s) to life?

You might consider the types of team building that Herminia Ibarra and Mark Hunter describe in their *Harvard Business Review* article "How Leaders Create and Use Networks." They say we have three types of teams working in our lives.

First, our Operational Network is composed of trustworthy colleagues who help us get the job done. This could be anyone who believes in you and cheers you on every step of the way. Second, our Personal Network is made up of people such as our mentors and coaches—they guide us from outside of our workplace to do a better job in our professions. For instance, your mentor might advise you to take a writing class so that you can contribute to the company newsletter and garner praise from the CEO. Third, our Strategic Network helps us look at the big picture of our careers, and they assist us in figuring out the next jump up the career ladder. For example, a member of your Strategic Network might say, "You're a great lawyer with awesome experience in the courtroom. Now it's time to campaign for that vacant position for judge on the Circuit Court."

These networks are crucial. They help us understand who is on our side and how they can help us connect with other folks to join our ladder-climbing team.

So build an indomitable team! List the people you will recruit to help you climb the ladder of success. If you already know them, great. If you need to meet them, figure out how to make that happen.

Be Where Important People Are

You do this, of course, through networking. If you want to network with important people you have to know where they are and get yourself there. Here are a few ways to do that:

+ **Power network within traditional channels.** Go to your company's events, where you get priceless face time with higher-ups. Follow up with notes. If you and an executive hit it off, ask her for help. Shadow her, ask for advice. Go to conferences, trade shows, banquets, and community events. Build your network upon the classic infrastructures of family, friends, your college alumni group, and professional associations. Be creative: frequent the jazz club or the gym where your future team members work out. Start an Internet newsletter. Connect with folks at the cleaners, the grocery store—everywhere.

+ **Join a networking group.** Find one whose members span every industry; that will give you a broad understanding of other businesses and exposure to new clients. If you're a Web page designer, join people who have companies that need your services. A good networking group will interview you, check your credentials, and charge a membership fee.

The ultimate networking group is eWomenNetwork. While the connections start online, the company hosts monthly events in 113 cities nationwide at which women can meet face-to-face to network, share ideas, and do business with each other. You can find networking groups within your specific field. For example, professional associations hold frequent functions, receptions, and lectures as catalysts for members to come together to meet, greet, and do business together. The best way to connect with a networking group is to start within your own profession—journalists, accountants, lawyers, doctors, massage therapists—they all have organizations, events, and conventions that offer amazing networking opportunities.

◆ **Connect with everyone.** That means networking up, down, and sideways. Don't think that to make the CEO chair by age forty-five, you should only interact with managers, VPs, and trustees. Build relationships with people in other companies and industries. Get to know the folks in the mailroom and the coffee shop, janitors, the newsstand operator, security officers—you never know who might offer a golden nugget of information that becomes your jackpot.

◆ **Find 'em!** Research where your dream team members work out, get coffee, and eat lunch. I am not advocating that you become a stalker, as that would defeat your purpose. After all, coming on too strong is a real turn-off in personal and professional situations.

However, if you become a friendly face in your potential dream team member's kickboxing class, and then ease into chitchat and get to know her slowly, you can ultimately introduce yourself as a business owner and propose that she consider joining your innovative venture.

Remind your potential dream team members of the power of teamwork. I always love to share one of my favorite Ethiopian proverbs: "When spider webs unite, they can tie up a lion."

Cast all conversations in a way that serves people. Speak about how your business can enhance their experiences and opportunities in the business world. Explain how you're offering a position to showcase their talents in ways that have never been done. Share the long-term benefits of getting on board a promising business and playing key roles when it's time for expansion. Make people understand that you will add tremendous value to their work if they join your team.

♦ **Serendipity rules!** Stay open to out-of-the-blue encounters that magically connect you with people you need. If serendipity is God's way of being anonymous, then it's no coincidence when the woman beside you at the bagel shop sees your company's logo on your baseball cap and "just happens" to be looking to partner with someone for her hot new venture. And it's not a "chance meeting" when a friend refers a man to your charity event and romance suddenly sizzles with him. Because when you're pursuing your passion, your positive energy attracts invisible forces in the universe that send good people to help you.

Cultivate Deep, Long-Term Relationships That Enrich You, Your Associates, and the World

If you lost your job today, who's the first person you would call? That's the point person in your network. Now name the next five people you'd contact. Consider: Do you spend about half your time nurturing these relationships by serving and adding value to these six people's lives? Truly successful people do that; you should write out a strategy to do so right away, because what you give, you get back a thousand fold.

Keep in touch by scheduling quarterly or monthly breakfasts, lunches, dinners, or coffee breaks. Almost half of us—49 percent—say restaurants are the top place for closing a deal outside the office, according to a *USA Today* survey of CEOs. Runners up: golf courses at 9 percent, trade shows or conferences at 7 percent, cars at 7 percent, sporting events at 3 percent, and aircraft at 2 percent. You can also make exercise dates or start a lunchtime motivational book club. Be creative.

I like to think of networking as gardening. Short-term networkers are doomed to plant seeds for quick-blooming plants that die just as fast. Long-term connectors plant seeds for deep-rooted plants that, when nurtured, bloom year after year. Be a connector.

Look at the Big Picture! Know that you are investing in a lifelong relationship. Appreciate that as the friendship deepens, so do business deals, in unexpected ways. For example, if during the era of record albums you connected with a record distributor, and then after a decade of win-win business interaction, CDs are invented—boom! Together you have a new product with more lucrative distribution potential. All thanks to your long-term relationship that has tilled the business terrain in a way that sprouts new and more valuable profits.

Exercise for Truth #10

If you're thinking, "I don't have a team!" then you're wrong! We all have teams playing the game of life right alongside us, every day. It's just a matter of identifying the members as such and implementing a game plan to optimize your wins.

So make a list of the people in your life in the following categories:

Family   Clubs

Colleagues   Place of Worship

Neighbors   Interest Groups

Classmates   Professional Associations

Professionals   Gym/Fitness Club

Community   Book Club/Golf Partners,
                                                etc.

Friends

Keep in mind that we can build a huge network of friends and associates who share our common ground, goals, and beliefs. I have 35,000 people in the FraserNet; I have connected with these men and women because they share my vision for networking and building great relationships in business and in life.

However, we click with only a small fraction of those people. The people we click with in our network are the folks that we stay in close contact with on a regular basis: our significant others, business partners, best friends, mentors, lovers, close clients, and so on. You can find the people I click with in my cell phone—all 655 of them—and they are listed on the dedication page.

And so, compile a similar grid of the men and women with whom you click and really think about what in those relationships served as the catalyst for your deep connection. The more you understand why you are drawn to and stick with particular people, the better you can cultivate those relationships to reach even deeper levels.

Next, as you build your business, identify the key players with whom you would like to connect and ultimately click. Make a list of men and women whom you need to meet; strategize how you will connect with them. Trust that the law of attraction will deliver the right people to you with the best chemistry, fit, and timing. And you will magically click with your team to live your dream!

Key **CLICK** Factors

Always

◆ Associate with people who are going or have been where you want to go.

Keep in Mind

◆ Shared interests are the basic building blocks of any relationship. Creativity and expertise matter most.

◆ When invited to the table of someone's life, bring something to the table or you may not be invited back.

Do Not

◆ Focus on what you can *get* from others; instead focus on what you can *do* for others.

Make Sure To

◆ Learn more if you want to earn more. List your unique skills, connections, and resources; then figure out who might benefit from a random act of kindness.

Resources

The Best Places to Click!

Locations, Groups, and Events
Volunteer activities
Professional conferences
Gyms and health clubs
Social events such as weddings, graduations, luncheons, and
  parties with friends
Beauty salons and barber shops
Alumni associations
Schools that your children attend
Cultural places and events such as museums, the opera, the
  orchestra, jazz festivals, art fairs, etc.
Bookstores
Reading groups
Religious institutions and events

Websites
Any website that's a community focusing on your interests,
including:
Cisforcupid.com (for romance seekers affected by cancer)
eWomenNetwork.com (women business to business, career
  development)

Facebook.com (college and workplace networks, music sharing to carpooling)

FraserNet.com (African American business, career, and economic development)

Irritatedbeingsingle.com (for people with Crohn's disease and
irritable bowel syndrome)

Linkedin.com (finding jobs, making deals, getting answers to
business questions)

Match.com (online dating, highly screened)

MySpace.com (social networking; core market is people in
their twenties)

Prescription4love.com (website for people with sexually transmitted diseases and other health conditions)

Secondlife.com (3-D virtual world built and owned by its
residents)

TEDtalks.com (discussion about technology and the Web)

ValentiInternational.com (matchmaking in the European
tradition)

Suggested Reading

Books

These are the books that have helped to shape my thoughts:

The 8th Habit: From Effectiveness to Greatness by Stephen R.
Covey (Free Press, 2004)

The 4-Hour Workweek by Timothy Ferriss (Crown, 2007)

The 7 Habits of Highly Effective People by Stephen R. Covey
(FranklinCovey Co., 2003)

25 Ways to Win with People by John C. Maxwell with Les Parrott (Thomas Nelson Inc., 2005)

212° The Extra Degree by Sam Parker and Mac Anderson (Simple Truths, 2006)

Awaken the Great Within by Anthony Robbins (Simon & Schuster, 2001)

The Coherent Heart by Rollin McCraty, Mike Atkinson, Dana Tomasino, and Raymond Trevor Bailey (HeartMath Research Center, 2005)

Cracking the Corporate Code: From Survival to Mastery by Price M. Cobbs and Judith L. Turnock (Executive Leadership Counsel, 2000)

Dig Your Well Before You're Thirsty by Harvey Mackey (Doubleday, 1997)

Five Major Pieces to the Life Puzzle by Jim Rohn (Jim Rohn International, 2000)

The Four Agreements by Miguel Angel Ruiz (Amber-Allen Publishing, 1997)

How to Succeed in Business Without Being White by Earl Graves (Harper Business, 1997)

How to Win Friends and Influence People by Dale Carnegie (Simon & Schuster, 1936)

How to Work a Room® by Susan RoAne (HarperCollins, 2007)

Kwanzaa: A Celebration of Family, Community, and Culture by Dr. Maulana Karenga (University of Sankore Press, 1997)

Lessons in Living by Susan Taylor (Anchor Books, 1995)

Life's Missing Instruction Manual by Dr. Joe Vitale (John Wiley & Sons, 2006)

Little Black Book of Connections by Jeffrey Gitomer (Bard Press, 2006)

Masters of Networking by Ivan Misner (Bard Press, 2000)

Never Eat Alone by Keith Ferrazzi with Tahl Roz (Doubleday, 2005)

The Platinum Rule: Discover the Four Basic Business Personalities and How They Can Lead You to Success by Tony Alessandra and Michael J. O'Connor (Time Warner, 1996)

The Power of Charm by Brian Tracy and Ron Arden (Amacom, 2006)

Reposition Yourself by Bishop T. D. Jakes (Atria, 2007)

The Secret by Rhonda Byrne (Atria Books, 2006)

Social Intelligence: The New Science of Human Relationships by Daniel Goleman (Bantam Books, 2006)

Stumbling on Happiness by Daniel Gilbert (Vintage Books, 2007)

Succeeding Against the Odds by John H. Johnson (Amistad, 1989)

Think and Grow Rich by Napoleon Hill (Ballantine, 1963)

Think and Grow Rich: A Black Choice by Dennis Kimbro and Napoleon Hill (Ballantine, 1991)

The Tipping Point by Malcolm Gladwell (Little Brown & Co., 2002)

Transforming Stress: The HeartMath Solution for Relieving Worry, Fatigue, and Tension by Doc Childre and Deborah Rozman (New Harbinger Publications, Inc., 2005)

Who Are You? by Stedman Graham (Hay House, 2005)

Magazines and Newspapers

Why read? You boost your click-ability quotient when you're informed. And you'll advance far beyond the sports and weather of Chit-Chat 101 to topics that fascinate and enchant others.

Daily: Your local newspaper, *USA Today*, and *The Wall Street Journal*

Weekly: *Sunday New York Times*, a weekly newsmagazine such as *Time, Newsweek, U.S. News & World Report, Business-Week*, and/or any publication that focuses on your specific career, business, or profession

Monthly: *O, Forbes, Fortune, Diversity, Inc., Vanity Fair, Fast Company, Inc., Entrepreneur, Self, National Geographic*

Annually: Six to twelve books, special edition "Year in Review" magazines, and the doctrine of your religion such as the Bible, the Torah, the Koran

Index

Clickin365

where your network increases your networth

VISION: To lead a values and principles-based global networking movement that teaches "netbuilding" and brings together diverse human resources, to increase opportunities for all.

MISSION: To promote and showcase our members'/partners' products and services and help them achieve their professional objectives. To create a networking culture centered on learning, "giving," and "adding value." To share with and provide our members unparalleled access to the people and resources they need to succeed.

CORE VALUES
We Value:
- Learning and growing
- Service to others as the foundation of success
- The importance of family and legacy
- Spiritual growth and guidance
- Building wealth honorably
- Being a positive role model
- A strong work ethic and loving what you do
- The importance of our relationships
- Making the investment to succeed
- Measuring success by the generational wealth we transfer

GUIDING PRINCIPLES
We Will:
- Put God first
- Foster trust through honesty and integrity
- Give first, share always
- Keep promises to ourselves and one another
- Treat everyone with dignity and respect
- Exceed expectations
- Practice listening as the first duty of love
- Use wealth as a force for good
- Think hard, work smart
- Practice humility as strength of character
- Give thanks in and for all things
- Live authentic lives
- Honor our work as a spiritual practice and as our gift
- Lead by serving

JOIN **ONE MILLION** OTHERS WHO SEE IT AS YOU SEE IT,
WHO WANT WHAT YOU WANT!
"**NETBUILDING**" AT ITS BEST
VISIT WWW.CLICKIN365.COM